The Unraveling of America

Stephen V. Monsma

wherein the author analyzes
the inadequacy of
current political options
and responds
with a Christian approach
to government

InterVarsity Press
Downers Grove, Illinois 60515

InterVarsity Press is the
book publishing division of
Inter-Varsity Christian Fellowship.

ISBN 0-87784-859-8
Library of Congress Catalog
Card Number: 74-14302

Printed in the United
States of America

To my mother,
Marie Vos Monsma

Contents

II. POLITICS IN AMERICAN SOCIETY

III. POLITICS IN THE WORLD POLITICAL ARENA

NOTES   213

Acknowledgments

To acknowledge all who helped in the writing of this book would clearly be impossible. I would, however, like to mention a few special debts. I am first of all indebted to the board and supporters of the Institute for Advanced Christian Studies and to the Earhart Foundation. A grant provided by the Earhart Foundation through the Institute for Advanced Christian Studies allowed me to take a year's leave of absence from my teaching in order to do the reading, reflecting and writing which resulted in this book.

I am also especially indebted to many of my colleagues at Calvin College for their stimulation, insights and perspectives which have no doubt influenced me even more than I realize. Among these, Paul Henry has been an especially valuable colleague and friend, with his gift for balancing encouragement and criticism.

Finally, I would like to explain that my dedicating this book to my mother is more than a traditional gesture made in a noble attempt to atone for past gray hairs given. Rather, it is a particularly fitting gesture. My mother combines—and has helped pass on to me—a deep Christian faith and a lively interest in the political and social worlds about her. And that is really what this book is all about. Christian faith—if it is truly deep—necessitates a lively interest in just such matters, for they greatly affect all persons. What content that interest should have and in what directions it should take us is the issue I explore in this book.

The Basics

I

1
The Unraveling
of America

FROM THE VANTAGE POINT of the mid-1970s it is difficult to re-
capture the sense of verve and energy, the feeling of purpose and optimism, which filled the nation in 1961 as John
F. Kennedy confidently grasped the reins of national
political power.

It was a glittering time. They literally swept into office,
ready, moving, generating their style, their confidence
—they were going to get America moving again. There
was a sense that these were brilliant men. . . .We seemed
about to enter an Olympian age in this country, brains
and intellect harnessed to great force, the better to
define a common good . . . the government had been
handed down from the tired, flabby chamber-of-com-
merce mentality of the Eisenhower years to the best and
brightest of a generation.[1]

By the end of the decade the glittering promises had turned
to ashes, the bright hopes to despair. The "best and the

brightest" had failed. Instead of a dynamic decade, filled with progress and ever higher levels of human achievement, the 1960s saw a rushing tumble of unsettling and traumatic events descend upon the United States: the assassination of John Kennedy followed by the assassinations of Martin Luther King and Robert Kennedy; the seemingly interminable war in Vietnam with its body counts and kill ratios; the burning, looting and killing in the black urban ghettoes; the campus riots and massive street demonstrations in reaction to the war and other perceived injustices; and the epidemic of illicit drug use and violent crime. The start of the decade, with its shining promises and bright hopes, seems light years away from its end, with national guardsmen shooting down students.

THE UNITED STATES IN THE MID-1970s

The tumultuous events of the '60s left their imprint on almost all aspects of American life. But the most consequential impact of the '60s was on American society's sense of confidence in itself and its institutions, purposes and future. Already in 1969 historian Arthur Schlesinger wrote of a "crisis of self-confidence":

> As the sixth decade of the twentieth century draws to a close, America is undergoing a crisis of self-confidence. For most of our national existence, we have enjoyed a placid faith in our virtue and our invulnerability. There have been dark days, but generally the storms pass quickly and the sun shines again. . . . We are a good deal less buoyant today about ourselves and our future. Events seem to have slipped beyond our control; we have lost our immunity to history.[2]

Since 1969 Americans' self-confidence has been further battered by events. The Watergate scandal revealed that some of the highest political officials in the land—perhaps even the President—were involved in burglaries, cover-ups, secret cash funds, bribes and lies. Spiro Agnew resigned the vice-presidency as a convicted felon; Richard Nixon resigned the presidency an admitted liar. The economy sagged under an unchecked inflation and an increasingly serious energy shortage. By the mid-1970s a sense of malaise hangs over the land. It touches on the ability of man to control himself and his world. Past answers have not worked: Wage and price controls have not stopped inflation; modern technology has not averted energy shortages; our structure of values has not prevented political corruption; and legislative action has not stopped environmental pollution or the effects of racism. What we are now undergoing looks very much like the unraveling of America.

This feeling of unease and uncertainty over mankind's direction was discussed in a *Time* essay: .

The reigning wisdom that informed and compelled the past few decades is under attack—or, at the very least under cross-examination. That wisdom has been variously called liberalism, rationalism, scientism: concepts certainly not identical but related. But now man's confidence in his power to control his world is at a low ebb. . . . At the heart of the ferment of the '70s is a deep, even humble perception that man and his universe are more complex than he recently thought. . . . Optimism had bred a false enthusiasm that this method or that system was somehow the answer. Now some of the growing skepticism questions whether any system can ever fully surmount the recalcitrance and perversity of man.[3]

The fact that self-doubts and a questioning of past values are indeed abroad in American society is demonstrated by the resurgence of interest in the occult and in religion (usually outside the established churches) and by the rise of nostalgia which looks back to an earlier age. It is also seen in the great popularity of three recent books which ques-

5

tion where man is going and what he is doing to himself: Charles Reich's *The Greening of America*,[4] with its critique of a materialistic set of values, Alvin Toffler's *Future Shock*,[5] with its emphasis on the unsettling effects of technological advance, and Richard Bach's *Jonathan Livingston Seagull*,[6] with its parable extolling independence and the breaking away from the confines of a narrow society.

On the political scene the malaise is reflected in the disenchantment many persons feel toward the traditional political spokesmen of both the left and right. To increasing numbers both the conventional left and the conventional right have failed. The latter has given us Watergate, uncontrolled inflation and a disregard for racial justice; the former has given us Vietnam, unworkable urban renewal programs and a war on poverty which has ended in surrender. No one seems to have a sense of direction.

As a result the public's sense of confidence in its political institutions and leaders has been shaken. As 1973 ended 53 per cent of the American people felt there was something deeply wrong in the land (compared to 39 per cent in 1968) and 71 per cent felt the federal government either had made their lives worse or had failed to improve them.[7] Between 1958 and 1972 those who declared they had little trust in the government doubled from 23 per cent of the population to 48 per cent.[8]

In light of these growing feelings of distrust and uncertainty, Christians are challenged to use the values and insights of Christianity to give direction to our confused age. Our society has tried humanism, scientism and existentialism—all of which have led us into a dead-end alley. The values and insights of a post-Christian world have given us body counts and kill ratios, the Damoclean sword of nuclear destruction and a technology which threatens all of us with dehumanization, presidential statements later declared "inoperative" and a felon as Vice-President, decaying cities and environmental pollution fed by an insatiable materialism. It is time that Christians speak to the political and social dilemmas of our society.

Yet Christianity is in danger of floundering in the political and social world with as little sense of purpose or direction as the various isms we have been following. When Christians have gained political and cultural ascendancy in the past, the record they have written has often been less than enviable. One thinks of medieval Europe with its crusades, rigid structure of privilege and persecution of Jews; or of Cromwellian England with its political authoritarianism and brutality toward Ireland. To give the direction our world so badly needs, a thoughtful understanding of Christianity's values must be wedded to an equally thoughtful understanding of the political and social worlds. Answers do not come easily and the pitfalls are many.

Yet the Christian—while recognizing his own fallibilities and limitations—is convinced his basic values and insights are true, and thus, when applied perceptively and accurately to the political world, will result in a surer sense of direction than will the non-Christian values and insights we have been following. Christianity does not offer a sure, self-evident way out of our difficulties; it does offer a better, more promising way than other approaches. I claim no more—or no less—for Christianity.

In this book I seek to analyze from within a Christian framework the basic nature and purposes of politics in human society, thereby seeking to point the way to government's playing a higher, more ennobling role in society than it is presently playing. Implicit in this effort is my belief that the assumptions, beliefs and ideals underlying our politics lie at the heart of what has gone wrong with our politics in recent years. To renew our politics we must renew our view of man, society and the role played by politics in society.[9]

A PLACE TO START

Since there are a number of somewhat differing traditions within Christianity, I should make clear what I take Christianity to be. First, Christianity is founded on the authority of the Bible; it asserts that the Scriptures are unique, having been inspired in a special way by God so that they are an infallible guide in faith and morals. Building on this biblical authority, Christianity proceeds to insist on the existence of a personal, sovereign God who broke into human history in the form of the God-man, Jesus Christ, in order to reconcile sinful man to himself and to establish his kingdom among men. The terms vary, but this conception of Christianity is usually called evangelical Christianity, sometimes also referred to as conservative, or historic, or orthodox Christianity.[10]

Evangelical Christianity is thereby clearly distinguishable from liberal Christianity, with its denial of the unique authority of the Bible and many of the historically accepted teachings of Christianity, and it is distinguishable—although less clearly so—from neo-orthodox Christianity, with its existentially influenced emphasis on personal crisis experience as the way to Christian truth.[11]

Evangelical Christianity has had a long and rich history. It traces its origins to the doctrines found in the Bible, most clearly developed by the apostle Paul in Romans and the apostle John in 1 John. It is the Christianity which was held by the early church, by the Protestant reformers and their followers, and is held today by many Christians in a wide variety of churches. It is the Christianity of the best-known doctrinal or creedal statements of the church down through its history: the Apostles' Creed, the Nicene Creed, the Augsburg Confession, the Heidelberg Catechism and the Westminster Confession. It is the Christianity of great historic figures in the church such as the apostle Paul, Augustine, Martin Luther, John Calvin, and John and Charles

Wesley. It is the Christianity of such literary figures as John Bunyan, John Milton, John Donne and C. S. Lewis. Today there are indications that evangelical Christianity represents the thought of "a larger number of Protestant clergy and laity than does any other theological position."[12]

It is this evangelical tradition in Christianity within which I stand and whose values and insights I will use to analyze the nature and purposes of politics in human society. On the basis of this analysis I will seek to reveal the sources of our current political difficulties and to point toward a new and better way. I thereby seek to provide an alternative to the political approaches spawned by the materialism, scientism, humanism and existentialism of our era and to the dead ends to which they have led us.

The rest of part I—chapters 2 and 3—sets down the basics, the primary ideas and concepts concerning the nature of man and politics necessary for a Christian perspective on our political problems. Then parts II and III apply the basic concepts and ideas developed in part I to the ongoing political world, showing how they reveal the weaknesses and problems of current approaches to policy making and point out a new and better way.

2
The Nature of Man

MORE BASIC TO POLITICS than laws and constitutions is man himself. It is, in the final analysis, men who write laws and constitutions, and men for whom laws and constitutions are written. Thus the necessary starting point for an understanding of a way out of our current political dilemmas is man: his nature, purposes and societal bonds. The nature and purposes—and shortcomings—of man's political life grow out of the nature and purposes—and shortcomings—of man himself. This chapter lays the groundwork for succeeding chapters by exploring the nature and purposes of man and the societies he has created.

MAN: HIS BASIC NATURE
There are basically two ways in which we can learn about man. We can observe mankind—and ourselves—and thereby learn about man in much the same way that we learn about any other physical object, such as a tree or

11

house. Or we can turn to the Bible. To the extent that our observations of mankind are accurate and to the extent that our understanding of biblical teachings concerning man is accurate, the conclusions we reach from these two sources will agree. These two sources of information about man— while different—are not antagonistic, but complementary. Each has something to contribute. The Bible, while true and accurate in its descriptions of man, is not primarily a book on anthropology and thus leaves many features of man underdeveloped or unexplored. And an observer of mankind cannot tell us about non-observable character-istics of man, such as his moral responsibility. Therefore, this section of the chapter draws upon both biblical and anthropological teachings in order to discover the basic nature of man.

Man as a Cultural Being
Basic to the Christian conception of man is the biblical teaching that man was created in the image of God. Genesis records, "So God created man in his own image, in the image of God he created him."[1] And herein lies—accord-ing to Christianity—the uniqueness of man.

Materially, there is no indication in Genesis that man is distinct from the rest of the created world. In fact, Genesis 2 specifies the rather ignoble material out of which man was formed: the dust of the ground. Observing mankind also tells us that man clearly possesses many characteris-tics in common with the animals with whom he shares this planet. Man's body bears many striking similarities to the bodies of animals. Man is bilateral (that is, his two lateral halves are symmetrical), as are most animals and all higher animals. His eyes operate on the same principle as do the eyes of animals. His reproduction process is similar to those of all higher animals. In fact, for almost every human organ, skeletal-muscular structure and biological process there is a counterpart found in most animals and certainly in all the higher animals.

Thus it is the image of God in man, not man's physical characteristics, which distinguishes him and raises him into a sphere distinct from all other living beings. But saying this leaves as much unanswered as answered. For what is meant by the image of God in man? What sort of unique qualities does its possession give man? The biblical answer to this question is not direct. The Bible contains no neat, clear definition of the image of God in man. As a result, at least part of the answer to this question—assuming, as Christian scholars have frequently done, that the image of God in man is that which distinguishes man from the animals[2]—rests on the observable differences between man and animals. And here the conclusions of anthropology are fairly clear.

Anthropologists have reached near consensus on the idea that the key mark distinguishing man from animals is man's possession of culture. David Mandelbaum, for example, has written:

> Culture distinguishes mankind from the rest of the animal world. . . . All men, of whatever kind and circumstance, have the capacity for using and developing culture. . . . There is no doubt that only mankind uses and transmits the capacities summarized under the concept of culture.[3]

Culture is here used in the sense it is defined in *Webster's Third New International Dictionary:* "The total pattern of human behavior and its products embodied in thought, speech, action, and artifacts and dependent upon man's capacity for learning and transmitting knowledge to succeeding generations through the use of tools, language and systems of abstract thought." Culture, in this sense, is man's ways of living, his patterns of behavior and thought.[4] Culture is marked by four characteristics which

13

flow out of the definition given above and which set it off as a unique attribute of human beings: It is learned and it is dependent upon man's ability to speak, to use tools and to reason.[5]

It is the last of these characteristics—man's reasoning ability—which underlies and makes possible the other three. Man has a super brain which sets him apart from all animals. Natural scientist Edmund Sinnott has suggested that culture arose when man's mind had developed to the point at which memory, reason and imagination were possible.[6] Sinnott described man's mind as a distinguishing mark:

> Man has emerged into a much higher behavioral level than any other animal can reach. His memory is far more extensive. . . . By seeking relationships between facts, he learns to recognize general uniformities and to relate particulars to them, thus acquiring ability to reason. He can prove that Socrates, being a man, must be mortal since all men are so. Thus he has come to deal in abstractions.[7]

James Orr, a turn-of-the-century evangelical theologian, in describing the image of God in man also stressed man's intelligence and reasoning ability as man's distinguishing mark:

> This self-conscious, personal life of man, however, is itself but a manifestation of something deeper—what we are accustomed to call *rationality*. . . . Yet reason in man, as a little reflection on its nature and results speedily shows, is something *qualitatively* different, and not merely different in degree, from what we find in animals. The difference is seen, for one thing, in this, that man alone possesses the power of *abstraction* and *generalization*.[8]

It is this mental development which has made possible the creation and use of language,[9] the ability to make and use tools and the capacity to transmit knowledge from one person and generation to another. It is this mental development which thereby makes culture—the distinguishing mark of man—possible.

The conclusion is that God's image in man involves, in part, man's cultural capacities and the reasoning abilities underlying them.

Man as a Creative Being

Scientists who have observed man differ on the exact extent to which man and his nature are determined by innate endowments and tendencies. Some stress the inherited traits and tendencies which they believe the natural selection process encouraged and etched into man's biological, genetic make-up during ages of evolutionary development,[10] while others stress the wide range of choices man is free to make in developing culture within the confines set by biology.[11] The difference is one of emphasis. Both sides recognize that both biologically inherited characteristics and learned patterns of behavior must be taken into account in order to understand fully man's cultures and actions.

Man, in short, is an active, creative being, yet he acts and creates within the bounds set by his biological inheritances. To create, as the term is being used here, is to mold, to shape, to form—whether what one is molding, shaping and forming is a painting, a musical composition, a law, a business, a skiing technique, a house, a meat sauce, a child's personality or one's own life. Creativity has been described by educational psychologist George Kneller:

In the most profound sense to be creative is to fulfill oneself as a person. Each of us is a unique pattern of potentialities; each of us gives to and receives from life something that will never be repeated. Moreover, each of us must either mold himself or allow external circumstances to mold him. The choice must be made again and again throughout our lives.[12]

It should be noted that the term *creativity* is being used here in a special sense. The essence of creativity is not simply innovation or originality. The dividing line between creativity and non-creativity does not lie between innovation and non-innovation, but between self-conscious, freely chosen action and unthinking, unself-conscious action. To create is to choose, to act, to make in a self-conscious manner. If one chooses, acts or makes in a manner similar to others before him, he is still being creative, so long as he is doing so because he has made a free, self-conscious choice. To create, in short, is to make—to make because one has freely and self-consciously chosen what to make and how to make it. To create is to act, not merely to react.

This creative capacity of man is made possible by the fact that in man instincts are relatively weak.[13] Man as a cultural being learns basic behavioral patterns, while animals are largely instinct driven.

Man is not the only animal who makes things. The beehive, the bird's nest, the beaver dam, and innumerable other structures in nature are products of animal manufacture. The difference is that man *learns* how to make things; unlike the bees he does not inherit the knowledge of how to do so.[14]

The point is that animals, because most of their behavior is instinctual, are not creative. Bees and beavers build everywhere the same houses—without ever even considering building different types of houses. Only man, because his house-building skill is learned, can freely choose whether to build the same type of house his parents had or to build a house better adapted to his environment or to build a different type of house for the sheer pleasure of doing something new. Only man is free to choose; only man is creative. Jonathan Livingston Seagulls are found among men, but not among seagulls.[15]

This creative capacity of man—this ability to choose and to shape and mold himself and his environment—is the driving force underlying culture. Culture changes and develops through the creative actions of innumerable individuals, within the bounds set, however, by man's inherited nature and tendencies.

The biblical conception of man assumes this creative capacity on the part of man. This is seen in the Genesis creation account, where God told man, "Be fruitful and multiply, and fill the earth and subdue it; and have dominion over the fish of the sea and over the birds of the air and over every living thing that moves upon the earth."[16] Man is to have dominion over creation; he is to act, mold and shape the world and all its creatures. In Genesis 2:19-20 one of the first tasks God gave man was to engage in the creative task of classifying the animals. As Udo Middelmann has accurately put it: "What we have here is God creating and bringing his creation to man so that man can categorize the environment in which he lives.... Man is the one who groups his environment into classes rather than being grouped by his environment into a class—man."[17]

In addition, the entire Bible assumes man is morally responsible for his decisions and actions. Such a responsibility makes sense only if man is a freely choosing, creative being. It would have made no sense for Paul to warn dogs, lions or horses: "For we must all appear before the judgment seat of Christ, so that each one may receive good or evil, according to what he has done in the body."[18] Biblical warnings about man's moral responsibilities for his choices and actions make sense only because man is a freely choosing, acting being. If man had no creative capacity —if he, as the animals, could not freely, self-consciously

17

choose and act—then to speak of moral responsibility would make no sense.

Thus Reinhold Niebuhr was fully biblical when he stressed the creative, self-determining nature of man:

Man is self-determining not only in the sense that he transcends natural process in such a way as to be able to choose between various alternatives presented to him by the process of nature but also in the sense that he transcends himself in such a way that he must choose his total end.[19]

If my argument is thus far sound, if culture is, in fact, the distinguishing mark of mankind and if creativity is the moving force underlying culture, then the conclusion is inescapable that in order to attain the fullest expression of what it means to be a person, one must be a willing, choosing, creative individual.[20] It is all too possible for men, even though endowed with a creative capacity, not to exercise that creativity, either because of their own actions or because of the loss of personal freedom. One thinks of the person who drifts along with the stream, conforming himself in an uncritical, unthinking manner to prevailing ideas and patterns of behavior. He merely yields to the predominate forces surrounding him. Such an individual is missing much of what it means to be a person, and even assumes some likeness to an instinct-driven animal, with his immediate environment replacing inborn instincts as the driving force. He has given up much of the joy and meaning of being a person.

The end result is not much different for the person who cannot exercise his creative capacity because of a loss of personal freedom. The slave, the prisoner, the subject under a totalitarian government—all have their ability to exercise creativity seriously truncated. They are denied much of what it means to be a person and under extreme forms of repression are reduced to near animal-like existence, with the drive of instinct replaced by repressive rules. Less frequently recognized is the fact that much the same results can be achieved when cultural or economic forces, such as extreme racial discrimination, total economic dependence on another person or an enforced poverty, afflict a person. Again one is being denied his ability to exercise freely his creative capacity; again he is being deprived of some of the meaning of being a person.

To attain the deepest and richest essence of being human one must be a culture-bearing, creative person. All men attain this essence to a degree, but some attain it to a fuller degree than others.

Man as a Moral Being

Christian thought does not stop, however, with identifying the image of God in man with man's creative, reasoning capacities. It also sees the image of God in man's moral sense. Man possesses the capacity—even the innate drive —to judge things as morally good or bad. Everywhere—in all societies—patterns of behavior, qualities of personality, and personal values are praised or condemned, approved or disapproved. Man is unalterably a religious-moral being. Moral judgments fill his literature, actions and traditions.

C. S. Lewis has written: "Human beings, all over the earth, have this curious idea that they ought to behave in a certain way and cannot really get rid of it."[21] Reinhold Niebuhr has described man's moral sense as "a sense of obligation toward the good, as their mind conceives it."[22] Anthropologist Walter Goldschmidt has observed that "within each social system there are certain overriding unities with respect to the idea of what makes a good man, a true man, a respectable man."[23] Christian and non-Christian scholars tend to agree on the existence of a moral sense in man, but to differ in that the non-Christian sees this moral

19

sense as simply an aspect of man's culture without any basis or legitimacy outside of man, while the Christian sees this moral sense as originating in God with a basis in God's universal will for man.

Man's moral sense, although distinct from his creative capacity, is closely bound up with it. Man's ability to be self-conscious, to step outside himself and look at and evaluate himself is what makes his moral sense possible.

It is this dual creative-moral ability of man that comprises the image of God in man, that makes man in a real sense God-like. He is a thinking, willing being able to make moral judgments. He is much lower than God himself. His mind is limited and, as we shall shortly see, his will and moral sense are corrupted. Yet he, among all living beings, has the ennobling status of being at least a pale reflection of God and his perfect intelligence and goodness. It is this which makes man, human life, of inestimable worth.

John Calvin wrote that the image of God in man, as originally created by God, consisted of "the perfection of our whole nature," and that man thereby possessed "a right judgment, had affections in harmony with reason, had all his senses sound and well-grounded, and truly excelled in everything good."[24] And the Christian political scientist, René de Visme Williamson, also captured it well:

He was made for freedom and immortality. He has imagination and partakes of the divine creativity. He differs from all other creatures in that he alone has transcendence. Man is part of his environment, but he also transcends it in that he can set himself apart from it, judge it, modify it, and remove himself to another environment. He is even self-transcendent in that he can look at himself as though he were somebody else and pass judgment upon himself with a surprising amount of objectivity. All these traits are attributes of divinity. They do not make him God; they do make him God-like.[25]

As originally created by God, man was a good, creative being in unsurpassed fullness and richness. He possessed the capacity for molding himself, his society and his environment in a harmony of true grace and beauty.

MAN: HIS BASIC PURPOSE

An exploration of man's purpose for existing starts with man's creative and moral capacities, which according to Christianity did not evolve by natural laws but were created and implanted in man by God. It would be strange indeed if God were to create a capacity in man which he did not intend men to use. This applies to all of man's physical properties. But as we seek out man's basic intended purpose, that which is distinct and central in man's humanness—the image of God in man—is of prime importance. Thus the Christian is driven to the conclusion that man's basic purpose must involve in one form or another man's properly using and developing his creative capacity and his moral sense.

It is vital to note that, although all men are born with a creative capacity and a moral sense, they can fail to make full use of their creativity and turn their moral sense in wrong directions. As seen earlier a person who merely reacts to his environment and conforms himself to prevailing attitudes and forces in an unthinking manner has in effect renounced much of his creative capacity. Even the highly creative person, however, can turn his moral sense —and thereby his creativity—in wrong directions. God not only created man with a moral sense, he also intends man to use that moral sense to choose good over evil, truth over falsehood, beauty over ugliness. Adolf Hitler stands as a representative of the highly creative person who dedicated his creativity to evil, falsehood and ugliness.

One can thus reasonably say that the basic purpose of man is to exercise and develop his creativity to the fullest in pursuit of that which is good and true and beautiful. But this leaves the obvious question of what constitutes the good, true and beautiful. By what norm are they to be defined? A Christian answers this question by turning to God's will revealed in Jesus' command to love God with all one's heart, soul and mind, and one's neighbor as oneself.[26] The latter half of this command is amplified and explained by the apostle Paul in his letter to the Christians in Rome:

> He who loves his neighbor has fulfilled the law. The commandments, "You shall not commit adultery, You shall not kill, You shall not steal, You shall not covet," and any other commandment, are summed up in this sentence, "You shall love your neighbor as yourself." Love does no wrong to a neighbor; therefore love is the fulfilling of the law.[27]

Man's basic, God-given purpose in life flows out of a combination of man's distinguishing marks—creativity and a moral sense—and the command to love God above all and one's neighbor as oneself.

Peter brought these ideas together in one passage when he wrote, "Above all hold unfailing your love for one another, since love covers a multitude of sins."[28] He then went on to stress—even though not using the word *creativity*—a Christian's obligation to show this love through the creative use of his abilities:

> As each has received a gift, employ it for one another, as good stewards of God's varied grace: whoever speaks, as one who utters oracles of God; whoever renders service, as one who renders it by the strength which God supplies; in order that in everything God may be glorified through Jesus Christ.[29]

It is all there: Man is to act creatively, guided by love, thereby bringing glory and honor to his Lord.

Thus I conclude: *Man's basic purpose is to exercise as*

fully as possible his creativity, guided by love for God and man. That is it. It is simple, yet the implications and applications are limitless. It means man should seek to explore new ideas, to develop his knowledge, to create things of beauty, to solve social problems, to seek peace, to purify his own heart, to develop his patience and all other virtues. Man, who biologically is closely related to animals and the rest of the world, is free—indeed has the destiny—to soar far above that world and all its creatures, seeking and finding the most enriching and beautiful goals of humanity in his creative and moral capacities.

MAN: HIS SOCIAL NATURE

Implicit in much of what is in this chapter is that man is a social being. What is implicit needs now to be made explicit. Man needs man. Without his fellow man, every person virtually loses his humanity.

Man performs almost every act in community with other men. The procreation and raising of children, work, recreation, worship—all are done in conjunction with others. The very fact noted earlier that man's instincts are weak and that he must learn patterns of behavior from others means that man must live in community. Physical survival requires it. In addition, every society is one generation removed from the jungle, in the sense that each generation must learn from scratch all that a culture or civilization has developed over the ages. Without that learning and the community necessary for that learning man would be back to his caves and stone tools.

But the social nature of man runs even deeper than the need to perpetuate civilization and survive physically. Psychologically a person needs the approval, affection and warmth of other humans. Persons without such human relationships tend to develop psychological problems which impair their normal functioning.

Individuals who have been deprived of a normal socialization experience have problems in both self identity (which is actually defined in terms of social identification with others) and group identity. In severe cases of isolation in childhood individuals become permanently impaired: they may be physiologically human but behaviorally are not quite so.[30]

Man's social nature is revealed in the account of God's bringing all the animals to Adam, with none being found a suitable companion for him (Gen. 2:18-25). It was not until God created Eve, thereby providing human companionship for Adam, that man's need for sociability was satisfied.

Man, in short, is a social being; and thus it is only in conjunction with other human beings that he reaches the full essence of humanity, that he can attain the distinctive human traits of creativity and morality. To be creative and to exercise that creativity in keeping with love for God and man—that is, to be fully human and to fulfill one's purpose in life—one needs his fellow man; he needs to live in human community. As we shall later see, the implications of this for man's political life are enormous.

MAN: HIS DISJOINTED NATURE

It requires no special insight to recognize that something is tragically wrong in the affairs of men. Man, that culture-creating, culture-bearing, reasoning being who was made in the very image of God himself and destined for a life of creative beauty and goodness, is everywhere bound in chains of hate, exploitation and violence. Man, created higher than the animals, time and again sinks lower than the animals. The long litany of sorrow and grief man has visited upon himself comes all too quickly and easily to mind: racism, war, murder, exploitation, lies and hate. From the gas chambers of Auschwitz to petty, small-town gossip man demonstrates his seeming inability to live with his fellow man in mutual respect and cooperation. An age threatened by death from both nuclear warfare and a natural environment poisoned by man's greed for material goods should hardly need to be persuaded that serious, persistent evils are bedeviling mankind.

Yet coexisting with hatred and self-aggrandizement one also finds joy, beauty and love. Two persons meet and a genuine concern and respect develops between them. A whole community rallies to meet a crisis in a spirit of mutual concern. The love and genuine sympathy between mother and child or between two young lovers reveals the potential that exists for goodness, joy and beauty among men.

Thus central to man's existence on this planet are two paradoxes. Man is capable of beauty and goodness—and seems to be instilled with a love of beauty and goodness— yet time and again he finds himself wallowing in a slough of hate and exploitation. Man knows goodness but seems irresistibly drawn to evil. He thereby all too often turns love to hate or indifference and mutual respect to self-aggrandizement.

This paradox leads to a second, parallel paradox. As seen earlier, man is an incorrigibly social being: Man needs man. Corresponding to this social nature of man is his attraction to the goodness, love and respect which makes community—social life—possible. But man's incorrigibly social nature is balanced by his inexorable attraction to evil. Man's achievement of true community is constantly thwarted by his own propensity toward evil: Estrangement, rather than community, is the bitter fruit. Man needs man, yet man cannot get along with man.

In this section of the chapter I wish to explore the source and nature of the evil which constantly thwarts man's attempts to grasp goodness and turns community into estrangement. I will do so at some length because one's view of society and of politics' role in society is profoundly affected by his view of evil in society and because I believe there has been a great deal of soft-headed and simply wrong-headed thinking on this question.

The Fact of Man's Disjointed Nature

There is universal agreement that there is something tragically wrong in the affairs of men. Many utopian books and essays have been written which have attempted to set down the source of man's troubles and the steps needed to eliminate them, but no one has ever claimed that utopia has already been attained. Men differ widely on the source of man's troubles—some find them in his economic or political systems, others in his social conditioning and his learning experiences, and still others in his own nature—but all agree that human society is plagued by troubles.

Christianity insists that the source of evil in the world lies within man himself—man's nature has become corrupted. Even though still capable of good, his nature is predisposed toward evil. Man was created good and perfect, but he has fallen into corruption. In addition Christianity insists that man is morally responsible for his evil, and therefore morally guilty when he does evil. This is the Christian concept of sin: Man possesses an innate tendency to perform evil, moral-guilt-producing acts.

In contrast to the Christian concept of sin are two other answers to the question of the source of the evil plaguing mankind. One finds the source of evil outside of human nature itself in man's social environment. The other agrees with Christianity in finding the basic source of society's evil lying within human nature, but differs from Christianity in attaching no personal, moral guilt to man's evil tendencies and acts.

Evil Originates in Man's Environment. According to the

first of these positions, man, whose essence is either naturally good or morally neutral, learns or is taught to do evil by environmental institutions or conditions. Jean Jacques Rousseau, for example, declared "that man is naturally good and that our social institutions alone have rendered him evil."[31] Rousseau, although his thought is highly ambiguous and in part self-contradictory, apparently envisaged a simple society, based on innocence and individual effort, as allowing the natural goodness of man to develop and grow.

> So long as men remained content with their rustic huts, so long as they were satisfied with clothes made of the skins of animals and sewn together with thorns and fishbones . . . in a word, so long as they undertook only what a single person could accomplish, and confined themselves to such arts as did not require the joint labour of several hands, they lived free, healthy, honest and happy lives.[32]

Robert Owen, a nineteenth-century Englishman, was also convinced that man is essentially good and that evil arises from ignorance and harsh living conditions. He argued: "In those characters which now exhibit crime, the fault is obviously not in the individual, but the defect proceeds from the system in which the individual has been trained."[33] Owen's thought has been summarized in this way:

> He was a prophet of the tradition of Rousseau; his gospel, the essential goodness of human nature. All wrong, all crime and suffering proceeded from the governments and other circumstances created by the perversity of man in the past. Let those governments be abolished, those circumstances re-created, give the natural instincts full play, and man would rise to his full stature and perfection.[34]

Karl Marx is a third example of a person who denied the

Christian teaching of the corruption of human nature and sought to find the source of evil outside of man. To him the source of evil resides in the capitalistic economic system and the deprivations spawned by it. Once man's economic needs are fully satisfied in the coming communistic society, crime will disappear and men will live in harmony, thereby permitting the coercive state to wither away.[35]

B. F. Skinner is a present-day example of one who finds the source of the current malaise to be outside of man. He locates the source of evil in man's general social environment. Man, we are told, "is indeed controlled by his environment."[36] Skinner refers "to practices in which a person is held responsible for his conduct and given credit for his achievements. A scientific analysis shifts both the responsibility and the achievement to the environment."[37] According to Skinner, once we accept the fact that human behavior is determined by environmental factors and not by resources of character and will within the individual human being, the way is open for the creation of a society of beauty and goodness. This can be achieved by manipulating man's environment.

> Physical and biological technologies have alleviated pestilence and famine and many painful, dangerous, and exhausting features of daily life, and behavioral technology can begin to alleviate other kinds of ills. . . . It is hard to imagine a world in which people live together without quarreling, maintain themselves by producing the food, shelter, and clothing they need, enjoy themselves and contribute to the enjoyment of others in art, music, literature, and games, consume only a reasonable part of the resources of the world and add as little as possible to its pollution, bear no more children than can be raised decently, continue to explore the world around them and discover better ways of dealing with it, and come to know themselves accurately and,

therefore, manage themselves effectively. Yet all this is possible. . . .[38]

In assessing the case of those who argue that evil in human affairs arises not from any defect in man himself but from man's environment, it is first of all necessary to note that this position clearly runs counter to the Christian conception. Jesus once declared to his disciples:

What comes out of a man is what defiles a man. For from within, out of the heart of man, come evil thoughts, fornication, theft, murder, adultery, coveting, wickedness, deceit, licentiousness, envy, slander, pride, foolishness. All these evil things come from within, and they defile a man.[39]

And the apostle James once wrote that "each person is tempted when he is lured and enticed by his own desire. Then desire when it has conceived gives birth to sin."[40]

Christian theologians have affirmed this. Augustine said, "The sin which they [the first men] committed was so great that it impaired all human nature—in this sense, that the nature has been transmitted to posterity with a propensity to sin and a necessity to die."[41] John Calvin spoke of man's "hereditary depravity and corruption of our nature."[42] Reinhold Niebuhr stated that man's will is corrupted and "that the root of man's lust for power and of his cruel and self-righteous judgments on his fellows is in himself and not in some social or economic institution."[43] Thus Christianity has, down through the centuries, insisted that the source of evil lies within man himself, within his own nature.

The Christian belief in the perversity of human nature has been strengthened by the witness of events and by observed patterns of human behavior. Societies have differed widely in their level of sophistication, cultural values and economic levels. In spite of the widely divergent environmental conditions these innumerable societies have created for their members, individuals in all of them have been marked by a host of undesirable traits—greed, selfishness, envy, violent tendencies and so forth. Throughout history there has been no lack of attempts to find the right combinations of societal conditions which will lead to happy, cooperative individuals, respectful of each other's welfare and rights. But none has succeeded. The efforts of all reformers have been thwarted.

Especially instructive in this regard are the nineteenth century's attempts to create small utopian communities, in which environments conducive to the development of joy, cooperation and respect would, it was anticipated, lead to truly united, prosperous societies. The smallness of these communities, their relative isolation from the outside world, and the thought and care that usually went into their planning would all indicate that if changing environmental conditions can eradicate evil from human society, it would have occurred in these communities. Robert Owen, who firmly believed in the basic goodness of man's nature and the possibility of creating good men by creating good environments, founded a number of communities based on his beliefs. All failed. In a speech in 1828 at the site of one of his experiments, New Harmony, he said,

> I gave leases of large tracts of good land for ten thousand years for a nominal rent, and upon moral conditions only; and these I did expect would have made progress during my absence; and now upon my return I find that the habits of the individual system were so powerful that these leases have been, with a few exceptions, applied for individual purposes and individual gain, and in consequence they must return again into my hands.[44]

A large number of other utopian, usually socialistic, communities were founded in both England and the United States in the nineteenth century. Time and time again these communities, in spite of their high ideals and noble aspirations, foundered on the rocks of dissension, apathy, personal greed and jealousies.[45]

So it has gone with all the great reformist and utopian movements of history. The French Revolution, sparked by the noble ideals of liberty, equality and fraternity, degenerated into the Reign of Terror and the Napoleonic Wars. The utopianism of the early days of the Russian Bolshevik Revolution proved disastrous and quickly gave way to more authoritarian regimentation. And even the social welfare reforms the modern western democracies enacted in the twentieth century have given rise to giant bureaucracies often as impervious to human needs as the conditions they were designed to alleviate. The record of utopian reformers—basing their reforms on the manipulation of environmental conditions—is one of dismal failure.[46] Thus the evidence suggests that we ought to look elsewhere for the source of the evil which continues to plague mankind. Christians say it is within his own heart that man should look.

Evil Originates in Man Himself. There is a second approach to the question of the source of evil in human society which is also non-Christian. It agrees with Christianity and differs from the approach just examined in finding the basic source of evil in society within man's own nature. This approach holds that as man evolved from lower forms of life certain innate behavioral tendencies, which may have been functional at one time in man's evolution, ceased to be functional yet continued to exist, plaguing man's attempts to build a good society. This approach is typified by the Austrian naturalist Konrad Lorenz and anthropologists Lionel Tiger and Robin Fox. Lorenz clearly sees the aggression drive in man as a part of his innate, inherited nature and as a drive which is presently malfunctioning to the point of being a disease.[47] He argues that

31

at an earlier stage in man's evolution man's strong aggressive drive was relatively harmless because man's ancestors did not have the physical means (such as claws or powerful teeth and jaws) to kill quickly. Thus man's strong aggressive drive was not weeded out by natural selection. But then man, with the sudden development of the ability to make lethal weapons, acquired the capacity to kill without any diminution of the aggression drive. Conflict, disruption and tragedy have been the results. This malfunctioning, innate aggressive drive, according to Lorenz, creates problems in many areas of human behavior.

It is self-evident that intra-specific [that is, within species] selection is still working today in an undesirable direction. There is a high positive selection premium on the instinctive foundations conducive to such traits as the amassing of property, self-assertion, etc., and there is an almost equally high negative premium on simple goodness. Commercial competition today might threaten to fix hereditarily in us hypertrophies of these traits, as horrible as the intra-specific aggression evolved by competition between warfaring tribes of Stone Age man.[48]

Tiger and Fox have concluded:

We cannot expect Utopias. *It is . . . natural to man* to create hierarchies, to attach himself to symbolic causes, to attempt to dominate and coerce others, to resort to violence either systematic or lunatic, to assert, to connive, to seduce, to exploit.[49]

Scholars such as Lorenz, Tiger and Fox are closer than Rousseau, Owen, Marx and Skinner to the Christian conception of evil in that they see something fundamentally wrong with human nature, whereas those finding the source of man's evil in man's social environment do not. Lorenz's words in the last paragraph of his book are almost identical to those used by Christian theologians to describe man's insoluble dilemma:

> The obvious conclusion is that love and friendship should embrace all humanity, that we should love all our human brothers indiscriminately. This command is not new. Our reason is quite able to understand its necessity as our feeling is able to appreciate its beauty, but nevertheless, *made as we are, we are unable* to obey it.[50]

Evangelical Christians and those seeking an explanation for evil in the evolutionary development of man differ in two respects. First, the Christians insist that man was created good, but fell into sin and therefore is morally responsible for the evil within him. The naturalistic explanation of the origin of evil sees man as never having been good and therefore as bearing no moral responsibility for the drives and inclinations left over from an evolutionary past. Second, Christians see man's nature as being corrupted in a deeper, more far-reaching sense than do those offering a naturalistic explanation. Nevertheless, for our limited purposes in this book, the agreement of Christians and naturalistic evolutionists is striking and significant. They agree that man's innate nature is corrupted in the sense that it is at war with the qualities of love, mutual respect and selflessness needed for a naturally cooperative, mutually supportive society. If one can accept this fact, whether he arrives at it via Christianity or via naturalistic evolution, he will accept the crucial fact that man—that wonderful, complex being with seemingly limitless potentialities—has indeed a fatal flaw in his nature.

The Essence of Man's Disjointed Nature

Man's corrupted nature has been mentioned numerous times on the preceding pages, but greater precision is needed. The preceding pages have sought to present the evidence in support of the Christian concept of sin, but the exact nature of that sin and the degree to which it has affected human nature are yet to be considered. This section considers the essence, or exact character, of man's corruption, and the next section the extent to which man's nature has been affected by this corruption. Sharpened insights into the nature and extent of human corruption will prove helpful in later chapters.

An understanding of the evil within man can perhaps best be gained from an understanding of its opposite—the goodness for which man was created.[51] Man was created good, and evil is the state that resulted when man lost this goodness. In this sense one can say that just as cold is the absence of heat so also evil is the absence of good.

Goodness, in Christian thought, is obedience to God, submerging one's will in God's will.[52] And what is God's will, God's law, to which he desires obedience? Jesus gave this answer to that question:

You shall love the Lord your God with all your heart, and with all your soul, and with all your mind. This is the first and great commandment. And a second is like it, You shall love your neighbor as yourself. On these two commandments depend all the law and the prophets.[53]

Perfect man would be man who wills to live in a harmony of love among God, his fellow men and himself. He loves all three. But only by loving God above all can a proper balance between love for fellow man and love for self be maintained.

The essence of the original sin of Adam and Eve—and this is true even if one does not accept as historical, as I do, the Genesis account of man's first sin—was their attempt to place their will ahead of God's will. Man's originally perfect love for God was permanently fractured when he consciously chose to do the very thing God had told man not to do. Man placed his will and his love of self ahead of

God's will and his love of God. This was the essence of Adam and Eve's sin—and of all subsequent evil.

Theologian James Orr expressed it well:

Here, probing the matter to its core, we seem to get at the real principle of sin. The principle of the good is love to God, subjection of the whole will to God. Sin in its essence is the taking into the will of the principle *opposite* to this—that not God's will, but my own will, is to be the ultimate law of my life. It is the exaltation of self against God: the setting up of self-will against God's will: at bottom *Egoism*.[54]

The essence of sin—of the corruption innate in man's nature—thus becomes pride, or love of self above all. Excessive self-love then leads to all sorts of evil. Paul in Romans referred to the heathen who "did not see fit to acknowledge God" and thereby

were filled with all manner of wickedness, evil, covetousness, malice. Full of envy, murder, strife, deceit, malignity, they are gossips, slanderers, haters of God, insolent, haughty, boastful, inventors of evil, disobedient to parents, foolish, faithless, heartless, ruthless.[55]

Elsewhere Paul described those who are enemies of Jesus Christ as those whose "god is the belly."[56] They worship their own appetites and desires instead of God. The belief that the essence of sin is pride or excessive self-love, and thereby rebellion against God, has been supported by a long list of Christian thinkers.[57]

Often the popular impression, both within and outside Christianity, is that the Christian concept of sin consists of what appears to be almost a random assortment of specific acts, with a strong emphasis upon illicit sexual acts and overt crimes against others, such as murder or robbery. But the true Christian concept of evil in man is more profound than that. Finding its essence in rebellion against God and the enthroning of self in place of God as an object of worship, sin, in its specific acts, reaches to a wide range of acts and attitudes. Paul in the words quoted above stressed qualities such as faithlessness, ruthlessness and hate as the chief fruits of sin. All are sins of the self against others, but they go beyond the entirely too narrow categories of overt acts such as murder and adultery. In another letter Paul gave another list of sins:

> Now the works of the flesh [that is, the results of excessive self-love or self-gratification] are plain: immorality, impurity, licentiousness, idolatry, sorcery, enmity, strife, jealousy, anger, selfishness, dissension, party spirit, envy, drunkenness, carousing, and the like.[58]

Again the list emphasizes underlying attitudes and outlooks which are broader and deeper than a few specific acts. The qualities listed do, however, work themselves out in specific acts: racial discrimination, economic exploitation, gossip or slander, and indifference to suffering, as well as the more often mentioned murder, robbery and sexual assaults.

One final point: Man's corruption is such that it tends to destroy community. By pride and excessive self-love man seeks to worship the self at the expense of others. In the process the bonds which hold a society together are weakened. All of the more specific sins Paul gave in the two lists quoted above work to destroy society or community. Community must rest on mutual respect for the integrity of the person; sin is the antithesis of mutual respect. Sin, therefore, is a corrosive agent eating away at the bonds of human society.

Elements of Goodness in Man's Nature

Christian writings seem to abound with gloomy references to man's totally depraved nature and to his irresistible inclination toward sin and all manner of evil. Yet simple observation tells us that there is goodness in man's relations with man. Love, peace, joy and beauty do exist. Men sometimes show mutual respect toward each other. They sometimes even risk their lives to save others. And the arts have created monuments of beauty—in architecture, music, painting, sculpture. Man's technology has built machines and structures which, while often ugly and destructive of the natural environment, have also sometimes been things of grace and beauty, relieving man of drudgery and pain while adding minimal pollution to the environment. The coexistence of evil with goodness naturally raises the question of the extent or pervasiveness of evil within the individual and thereby within society as well.

Evangelical Christianity, because it historically has often had to fight against overly optimistic assessments of man's nature, has tended to develop at length its teachings concerning man's sinfulness, but has paid less attention to the elements of good still remaining. Therefore some observers have concluded that Christianity holds to a view of unrelieved pessimism concerning man's capabilities and potentialities. But this is not the case. Christianity teaches that God did not simply abandon man to his excessive self-love and its bitter fruits, but continues to act in history to limit the extent of sin and to redeem man from his course of love of self above all.

Even John Calvin, supposedly the Christian thinker most pessimistic and somber concerning man's goodness and potentialities, wrote:

> In every age there have been persons who, guided by nature, have striven toward virtue throughout life. . . . They have by the very zeal of their honesty given proof that there was some purity in their nature. . . . These examples, accordingly, seem to warn us against adjudging man's nature wholly corrupted, because some men have by its prompting not only excelled in remarkable

deeds, but conducted themselves most honorably throughout life.[59]

And theologian Charles Hodge, a follower of the supposedly gloomy Calvin, once wrote: "The Scriptures recognize the fact, which experience abundantly confirms, that men, to a greater or less degree, are honest in dealings, kind in their feelings, and beneficent in their conduct."[60]

But Christianity argues that the virtue and goodness we observe in man are there because God is actively restraining sin in man, not because man by his own powers is resisting the slide into the slough of absolute corruption.[61] This means that the goodness we observe in man is real and present, but still is not meritorious in the sense of being of moral worth in God's sight. Nevertheless the important point for our purposes is that elements of goodness have been preserved in man.

Thus all men possess a mixture of good and evil, light and darkness, with the proportions of good to evil, light to darkness varying greatly from one person to another. There are also societal differences, with some societies marked by a higher level of respect for the integrity of the individual and a greater compassion than are others.[62]

Yet in saying all this one must remember that man, and therefore society, is inclined toward evil. It is easy to slide into hate, fear and envy, and difficult to climb up to love, respect and cooperation. This is as true of societies as it is of individuals.

This then is the raw material with which governments work. Of all the facts related to politics one is clear: Politics operates down in the very practical, grubby world of real people and real societies. Governments are integral parts of societies, and it is out of the nature of man and his societal life that the basic nature and purposes of government emerge. This is what the next chapter is all about.

3
The Nature
of Politics

MAN NEEDS MAN; yet man cannot get along with man. The truth of this paradox, seen in the previous chapter, is basic to an understanding of the role of politics in human society. Man is a social being: He is dependent upon his fellow man for this physical survival and for the development of his cultural and creative capacities. It is only in community with other men that man is able to achieve his full potential for a meaningful, creative life. But man's achievement of community is constantly thwarted by his own sinful nature, by his own excessive self-love, which constantly places self-gratification ahead of the mutual love and respect on which community must rest.

Yet the paradox of man's needing man and man's not getting along with man is not fully accurate in one respect. Man is not at total enmity with his fellow man; he is not totally dominated by self-love. Therefore some basis remains for community—imperfect, fractured community, but community nonetheless. To a severely limited degree man can in fact get along with man.

It is out of this setting that politics is made both necessary and possible. If man were perfect, politics would not be necessary; if man were totally without goodness, politics would not be possible. If man were marked by love of God and therefore by a proper balance between love of self and love of others, government—at least as we now know it—would not be necessary. Man, following his nature, would live in love and respect without the need for the constraints of government. As James Madison wrote in *The Federalist*, "But what is government itself, but the greatest of all reflections on human nature? If men were angels, no government would be necessary."[1] But if man were wholly evil, guided wholly by self-love, government would not be possible. Politics must rest on a certain measure of trust and good will among men, without which no government can long survive. Basic to the analysis of this chapter is this understanding of man as an imperfect but not absolutely evil being.

In the following section I analyze the basic nature of government and politics. Later in the chapter I analyze the role government and politics play in human society, taking into account both the nature of man and society and the nature of government and politics.

GOVERNMENT AND POLITICS

Let me tell you a story about two men, both of whom suffered a misfortune one evening. The first man decided that since it was a delightfully cool night he would go for a stroll in a nearby park before retiring. But while he was strolling in the park, a thief leaped out from some bushes, held a gun against his back and demanded his money. Unfortunately our victim had just cashed a fairly substantial check and was carrying a hundred dollars in cash. The thief quickly took this money and made his escape before any help could arrive. Our victim went home a poorer man.

A second man that same evening was struggling with his annual income tax forms. He figured and refigured columns of numbers, but each time he came to the same conclusion—he owed the government an additional one hundred dollars in taxes. Finally giving up in disgust, he reached for his check book, wrote out a hundred dollar check, stuffed it and the appropriate forms into an envelope and mailed them off to the government. He too went to bed that evening a poorer man.

Superficially, these two men suffered similar fates: Both gave up a hundred dollars they desired to keep for their own use, and both acted under coercion, or the threat of sanctions (the gun and physical harm in one case and fines and possible imprisonment in the other). In other words, both the gunman and the government possessed power over their respective victims; both were able to force their victims to do things they otherwise would not have done.

Authority and Legitimacy
In spite of these similarities, however, a fundamental factor distinguishes the two events. The man who lost his money to the thief never for a moment would imagine that the thief had a right to demand the money and that he had an obligation to give it. It was a matter of physical coercion, pure and simple. In the case of the tax-paying citizen, he probably would acknowledge, even while wishing he could keep the money, that the government possessed the right to demand taxes and that he had an obligation to pay.

Thus both the gunman and the government possessed power, but their power was of quite different kinds. The gunman's power rested on naked, physical coercion; the government's on feelings of obligation and "oughtness." Or, to use the terms political scientists use, the government possessed *authority* and the taxpayer accorded the government *legitimacy*. To accord *legitimacy*, as the term is being used here, is to accept as fact both the right of another person or institution to command one's obedience and the existence of one's obligation to obey these commands. *Authority* is the capacity of a person or institution to command obedience in others because of the legitimacy accorded that person or institution by others.[2]

In our story the thief's victim accorded the thief no legitimacy and thus the thief possessed no authority over his victim. Physical coercion was the only relationship between them. On the other hand, the taxpayer accorded the government legitimacy—he recognized the government's right to charge taxes—and thus the government did possess authority over him.

As just seen, the government-governed relationship is an authority relationship. There are many other authority relationships. The relationship of employer to employee, parent to child, teacher to student and military officer to enlisted man are all marked by authority, with the employer, parent, teacher and officer normally accorded the right to command obedience (within circumscribed areas) by the employee, child, student and enlisted man.

One final note—the authority possessed by and the legitimacy accorded to persons and institutions can be either proper and rightful or improper and indefensible, as judged by standards or values outside the authority relationship. Authority and legitimacy, as the terms are being used here, are purely descriptive terms and make no pretense of evaluating the propriety of the authority relationship. Whether or not, in any particular case, persons ought to be according legitimacy to a person or institution—thereby conferring authority upon him or it—is a separate question.

When Adolf Eichmann, one of the key persons in Nazi

Germany's extermination of millions of Jews, pleaded innocent to any criminal guilt, saying he was merely following orders, he indicated that he had accorded legitimacy to his superiors no matter what orders they gave. Thus his superiors possessed absolute authority over him. Most persons today would argue that, based on standards of humanity and decency, his superiors had no right to give him such orders and he ought to have rejected the legitimacy of those orders. But this does not alter the fact that Eichmann's Nazi superiors did in fact have authority over him and that their orders were legitimate in that Eichmann accepted them as such.

By the same token, there can be situations in which persons—again according to outside standards—ought to confer legitimacy upon a person or institution, but fail to do so. Authority then should be present, but it is not, as perhaps in the frequently observed case of a son who fails to accept his father's right to regulate the use of the family car.

With this consideration of the nature of authority as a background, we can now consider the exact nature of governmental, or political, authority.

Political Authority

As is clear from the earlier discussion, governments possess authority, or, looking at it from the perspective of the citizen, are accorded legitimacy by their citizens.[3] Most present-day political scientists give these elements of authority and legitimacy a central place in their definitions of government or the political. What they then need to do is to distinguish the authority of what is usually called the government from the authority of other societal institutions. To do so is not easy. The government shares many characteristics with other governing authorities. In fact, to possess authority essentially means to govern—to make decisions which one expects to be obeyed because of the authority he possesses.

What distinguishes the government and the political from college, church or group governments is the society-wide nature of its authority.[4] The government possesses the right to command obedience from all members of an entire society. Its authority is limited in its depth—there are certain areas in which the government has no right to demand the obedience of its citizens—but its authority is not limited in its societal scope. The government has a right to demand obedience of all members of a given society. A parent's authority stops with his children, a church's with its membership, a teacher's with his students, but the government's authority is as wide as society itself. Thus the government can be defined as the social institution which possesses the right to make authoritative decisions for an entire society. The term government will be used in this book to refer to this institution with society-wide authority. When the governments of subsocietal organizations are being referred to, this fact will be clearly stated.

A concept closely allied to government is politics. Politics, as the term is used in this book, is the process of making authoritative decisions for an entire society. Thus the government is an institution and politics is what goes on within that institution.[5] But in both cases the key, distinguishing element is the making of authoritative decisions for an entire society.

This consideration of government and politics reveals something of their basis and nature, but does not reveal their God-given role in human society. That all-important question remains to be answered. But before doing so, we must first consider the nature of freedom, a concept crucial to the understanding of the purpose of government and politics.

44

FREEDOM

Freedom is one of those words which has been used and misused to the point that it communicates very little. In today's world freedom—whatever it is—is considered to be something good. Thus the word is often used for propagandistic purposes, with the speaker assuring his listeners that whatever he is offering (from a new automobile to a new political program) will result in more freedom for them. Clarity concerning the nature of freedom is the first casualty. Yet clarity concerning the nature of human freedom is essential to an understanding of the role politics plays in human society, since the role of politics is tightly bound up with freedom and allied concepts such as order and justice. In seeking out the actual nature of personal freedom, or liberty,[6] the best starting point is to consider absolute freedom and why true freedom cannot be equated with it.

Absolute Freedom

Absolute freedom can be defined simply as the option of doing, saying and thinking whatever one wishes to do, say or think. No one or no thing ever limits one in any manner. To see the inadequacy of equating this concept with actual freedom, it is important, first, to note that there are at least six major sources of limitations upon our freedom.[7]

One source of limitations is the general mores, or customs and traditions, of our society. There are certain acts which none of us, or almost none of us, would think of doing, not because they are illegal and not because we might not like to do them, but because society proscribes them. Most of us would not wear a swimming suit to a Lincoln Center concert or eat pork chops with our fingers in a restaurant or walk down main street singing at the top of our lungs, even though at times such activities might be more comfortable, convenient or fun than refraining from

45

them. The threat of ridicule, scorn and social ostracism and certain learned internal feelings of embarrassment are society's means of achieving conformity to innumerable social conventions. Normally they are so much a part of us that we give them little thought. Nevertheless absolute freedom is thereby compromised.

Our freedom is also compromised by the social groups of which we are members. Labor unions, professional associations, churches, country clubs, families, groups of mutual friends and places of work, such as offices and factories, are examples. All groups have at least some rules (written or unwritten) they expect their members to obey, and many have numerous, intricate regulations. The labor union member who does not wish to go out on strike, the physician who wishes to perform unnecessary operations, church members who wish to live in adultery, country club members who wish to dine in sweat shirts and blue jeans, teen-agers who wish to stay out all night, persons who borrow money from their friends without paying it back and workers who wish to come to work at 10:00 A.M. are all examples of group members who are likely to run into conflict with the standards of their groups. Sanctions such as fines, restricted rights, loss of friendships, or—normally the ultimate penalty available—expulsion from the group are the likely consequences. The important point for our purposes is that every person is a member of some groups and that all groups limit, in some way, his liberty to do, say and think whatever he pleases.

Our freedom is also limited by other individuals and by groups of which we are not members. Sometimes these limitations take violent forms, as when a thief steals our money at gunpoint or the Mafia extorts a kickback by threatening physical harm. Our liberty is clearly being limited in such cases. But it is also limited by gentler means. A large corporation constructs a gas station next to our house, and the peace and quiet we desire is denied us. Or our neighbor throws his garbage into his back yard, and the subsequent stench and health hazard created deprives us of our freedom to enjoy an odor-free, healthy environment. Examples could be multiplied indefinitely. Time and again the actions of one individual or a group severely affect other individuals, thereby placing limitations on what they can do, say or think.

A fourth way in which our freedom is limited is by the government. All persons live under some form of government, and all governments impose certain rules and regulations upon their citizens. Absolute freedom is thereby again restricted.

It is also helpful to note that absolute freedom is limited by an individual's physical limitations. Someone may wish to become a professional basketball player, but if he is only five-feet-six-inches tall, he is unlikely to succeed. Or a person may wish to climb a certain mountain, but a weak heart prevents him. Or a married couple may desire children of their own, but because of certain physical abnormalities may be unable to have them. The point is that all people possess certain physical characteristics which keep them from doing certain things they really wish to do. Once more absolute freedom is limited.

Finally, man's liberty to do whatever he pleases is limited by what are often called *acts of God* or *acts of nature*. Natural disasters such as floods, tornadoes, hurricanes and earthquakes often affect individuals, forcing them to make choices they do not wish to make. Or on a less serious plane, a carefully planned picnic may have to be cancelled because of rain. Again human freedom is being limited by forces outside a person's own will and desire.

The conclusion is that every person is surrounded by a host of forces—social, political and natural—which at almost every step channel and limit his choices. Absolute freedom, in short, does not exist. Absolute freedom for man is, in fact, of necessity an impossibility. To live in society man's freedom must be limited. A's freedom to drive his sports car at ninety miles an hour through a residential area is a denial of B's freedom to a safe and peaceful neighborhood. In fact, one can go beyond this and pose the paradox that absolute freedom means no freedom. If everyone could do whatever he pleased, everyone would be free to act in ways which limit others' freedom. Chaos with no freedom would be the net result.

All persons live under societal mores, are members of groups, are affected by other persons and groups, and live under government; all persons, therefore, find their freedom limited. But what about the hermit who lives completely by himself? He is not a member of any society, is a member of no group, is in contact with no other person or groups and is subject to no government. Is he not then absolutely free? He still is, however, restricted by his own physical limitations and by forces in nature. Were it not for these, one might agree he would be absolutely free, but he would no longer be human. Man is a social being and without his fellow man he cannot learn speech, culture, rational thought and creativity, which are the distinguishing marks of man. Thus we conclude that to be human means to be limited in what one can do, say and think. Absolute freedom is a mirage. The concept of true personal freedom must be based on a more realistic view.

Freedom, Order and Justice

True human freedom as an ongoing, actual possession of man cannot be absolute freedom—complete freedom to do whatever one pleases. This much is clear. But this basic fact raises the difficult question of how, or according to what principles, ought human freedom to be limited. Freedom, at the very least, implies open, discretionary choice, while limitations imply the closing or restricting of free choice. Limited freedom appears to be a contradiction in terms.

Rights-Obligations. The starting point for finding a way out of this dilemma is the recognition that every human being possesses certain rights simply because he is a human being. *Rights* are here referred to as simply one's due—that which justly accrues to or is due a person. The history of western thought is rich in positing the existence of certain natural rights inherent in mankind. This concept was particularly central in the thought of the Greek Stoics, the medieval scholastics and the eighteenth-century rationalists. As the American Declaration of Independence proclaims, "We hold these truths to be self-evident, that all men are created equal, that they are endowed by their Creator with certain unalienable Rights, that among these are Life, Liberty, and the pursuit of Happiness."

But in the twentieth century the reigning wisdom in most of western thought, under the influence of positivism and derivations of it, has insisted that man has no natural rights. His only rights are those given him either by cultural customs and conventions or by laws enacted by some government. Positivism, with its belief that man evolved by a natural process from lower forms of life and originally from nonliving material, has no basis for seeing man as other than an exceptionally complex configuration of molecules and electrons. Man may be more complex, but in essence is no different than a stone, tree or dog. He is purely material, and to speak of inherent worth or rights is impossible, for the existence of anything nonmaterial beyond man has been excluded at the start.[8]

The trouble with this approach is that it flies in the face of our own experiences. We may speculate theoretically about whether man has inherent worth and therefore also inherent rights, but deep in our hearts each of us believes that he is no mere blob of protoplasm. Man experiences pain and pleasure; he tastes life; and he knows that he possesses worth and rights simply by virtue of his humanity. He may not be able to prove it, but he has no need to; he feels and experiences it himself.

Christianity, in contrast to positivism, has consistently been in agreement with man's own personal experience in asserting that man by virtue of his humanity has an intrinsic worth and therefore also certain inherent rights.[9] The basic source of the differences between positivism and Christianity lies in the fact that, as noted in the previous chapter, Christianity insists man was created in the image of God and destined for a life of creative joy. These concepts of necessity carry with them the existence of individual rights. A being created by a personal God and given a unique, God-like creative capacity surely has an intrinsic worth and thereby intrinsic rights as well. In addition, man's creativity takes on meaning only to the extent that he possesses certain rights which will ensure that he will be able to exercise his creativity. An individual whose every choice is determined by irresistible forces—governmental, economic or whatever—has lost his rights, and therefore also the ability to exercise his creative capacity.

What is sometimes not recognized is that rights and obligations are two inseparable sides of the same coin. My right to life is secured by your obligation not to kill me. This reciprocal relationship holds true for all rights. Every right is secured by one or more reciprocal obligations imposed upon society. One person's right to freedom of religion is secured by the obligation of other individuals and groups, as well as the government, not to interfere with the free exercise of religion. One person's right to a clean, healthy physical environment is secured by all persons' obligation not to contaminate the environment. In short, all rights carry with them corresponding obligations.

Thus far I have stressed rights and obligations which inhere in man simply because of his humanity. They are there, whether or not any particular individual, society or government recognizes them or seeks to order themselves in accord with them. These are the most basic, far-reaching rights and obligations. But specific governments (and more about the role of government in all this in a little while) enact laws which also specify rights and obligations, but of a nonfundamental nature. A city, for example, may decide it wishes to preserve an old section which has many homes of historical significance. The right of the citizens of that city to the possession and enjoyment of a historically significant section is thereby secured by the obligation of homeowners in that section not to tear down their homes and of developers not to bring commercial establishments into that area.

In some ways rights and obligations of this sort could better be called advantages and disadvantages. One is not dealing with rights in the sense of something due one because of his humanity. Rather they are given one by a government because they were judged advantageous to society. On the other hand, they could still legitimately be considered rights because they help make possible a creative life. Without them man and society could survive, but life would be less free, less full. Since man was created for a full, rich, creative life, that which helps make such a life possible is truly due him, is truly a right. But in order to distinguish these rights from basic, inalienable rights, I will refer to them as convenience rights or advantages.

Thus each individual is surrounded by a host of rights and obligations, and advantages and disadvantages, some of which inhere in him simply because of his humanity (basic rights) and some of which are imposed because of the political authorities' judgment of their advisability (convenience rights or advantages).

True Freedom. Now it is possible to come back to the central issue: the nature of true human freedom. The existence of rights offers a basis for the safeguarding of a large measure of freedom. To the extent man's basic rights are recognized and respected man is free to express his beliefs, to worship God as he sees fit, to pursue the occupation he desires, to form social groups and to live where he wishes. And to the extent convenience rights or advantages are provided, man's life is made more secure, challenging and meaningful. But what must also be recognized is that as rights are expanded and protected, obligations and disadvantages, which restrict an individual's free choice, are also expanded. The very acts which expand freedom also contract it.

The only way out of this dilemma is to discover some criterion by which competing rights and obligations can be ranked. Then we would be in a position to answer the crucial question of whether or not the protection of right X is worth the imposition of obligation Y. Or, to give a concrete example, is safeguarding the rights of blacks (or some other minority group) to purchase houses wherever they please and are financially able worth the imposition of the obligation on homeowners and realtors to sell houses to all qualified buyers regardless of race, color or creed?

In finding a criterion with which to rank and evaluate competing rights and obligations the concepts concerning man and freedom thus far developed are most useful. They lead to a criterion which seeks to assure the fullest opportunity for man to develop his essential humanness. In the previous chapter, I argued that God created man in his image and that this image of God in man consists of man's moral sense and his creative capacities as a thinking, creating, willing being. Man is destined to be a shaping, forming, molding being—in short, to be *creative* in the fullest and richest sense of that term.[10] In exercising this creativity man should be guided by love for God above all and by love for his fellow man and himself. Man thereby fulfills his God-given destiny as a man.

Thus man's central God-given purpose as a creative, moral being should form the basis of the criterion by which we sort out which rights are more important for man, and therefore should be safeguarded, and which ones are less important, and therefore can be sacrificed in the achieving of more important rights. Then true freedom would be defined as that condition under which man has the greatest opportunity to exercise and develop his creative capacity in keeping with love of God and man—the essence of the image of God inherent in him.

Achieving this sort of freedom can then become the criterion by which rights and obligations are apportioned within a society.[11] Those rights and obligations should be recognized which maximize true freedom, that is, which achieve the greatest opportunity for individuals in society to develop and exercise their creative capacities, guided by love of God and man. To achieve this true freedom society must engage in a balancing process, weighing the expansion of freedom resulting from safeguarding a certain right against the contraction of freedom resulting from the imposition of the obligations necessitated by the safeguarding of that right. In striking this balance the number of persons gaining freedom versus the number losing freedom as well as the significance and value of the freedoms being gained and lost must be weighed. True freedom in society is increased when more persons rather than fewer persons are given opportunities to act creatively in love; true freedom in society is increased when persons have the opportunity to act in more important ways in keeping with love of God and man rather than in less important ways in keeping with love of God and man or not in keeping with love of God and man at all.

To take a particularly clear example, weighing the right of women to safety from sexual assaults versus the right of potential rapists to act out their sexual violence, it is clear that the imposition of the obligation not to assault and the safeguarding of the right to safety from assaults results in an overall expansion of true freedom and helps make society possible. More persons desire to be free from sexual assaults than desire to assault sexually, and, much more importantly, being free from assaults is vitally important in making possible a creative, loving life, while the "right" to assault is not at all in keeping with love of God and man (and thus the obligation not to assault really does not at all limit one's opportunity to act creatively in love).

The weighing process that must go into maximizing true freedom in society can also be seen in the area of work and occupations. If someone or some outside force could coerce me into a particular occupation against my will, I would be losing a crucial freedom: the freedom to choose, free from unreasonable, arbitrary restraints, in what sort of activities I will spend my time earning my income. If I am unable to choose freely whether to be a farmer or teacher, artist or assembly line worker, I have lost a crucial means of living a creative, loving life. On the other hand, the ability for me to dictate others' occupations is really not a crucial means of fulfilling my creative, loving purpose as a man; it is not a crucial freedom. On a scale based on God's law of love, freedom to choose one's own occupation clearly must be ranked higher than the freedom to dictate the occupation of others. In addition, thwarting individuals who desire to dictate the occupations of others would affect only a few persons, since only a few desire to do so anyway. I therefore conclude that on balance true freedom in society is increased by everyone's having the right to choose his occupation free from arbitrary, unreasonable restraints—even at the expense of imposing the obligation on everyone to refrain from attempts to dictate the occupations of others. Other examples, some of which are much more controversial than these two,[12] come readily to mind, but the basic criterion should be clear: to maximize true freedom in society.

Conceiving true freedom in terms of maximizing man's opportunities to exercise and develop his creative capacities does not mean groups become unimportant. Since man is the social being that he is, he will often choose and in fact sometimes will only be able to achieve his desired goals through forming groups and acting in conjunction with others. Thus maximizing true freedom includes the maximizing of individuals' freedom to form and work through groups. The freedom of groups such as churches, business associations and social clubs is thereby protected. If someone were, for example, to prevent my church from holding worship services, my personal freedom to worship God as I see fit would be limited.

In all this one must keep in mind this paradox: To maximize true freedom it is necessary to limit personal freedom. To maximize true freedom is not to embrace absolute freedom. As noted earlier, if everyone could do whatever he pleased, no one would be free. Thus maximizing true freedom requires striking a balance between allowing free choice and curtailing free choice. This balance does not spontaneously arise in society, but must be sought by a self-conscious, painstaking process. Here is where government and politics enter in. But more on that shortly.

When freedom is maximized by a proper balance between granting and limiting free choice, man becomes free to act as the creative, moral being God intends him to be. He is able to create—to mold and shape himself, others and his physical environment, and in so doing he is able to choose as a responsible agent. Yet he is not completely free. There are obligations he must observe if his fellow members of society are to enjoy the same freedom he enjoys. He buys his personal freedom by respecting the rights of others, by accepting limitations on his freedom.

Justice and Order. The concepts of justice and order emerge out of the above discussion. *Justice* is the apportionment of rights and obligations which maximizes true human freedom. This concept of justice rests on the age-old concept of justice as giving each man his due, as according each man his rights. But, as I have stressed all along, obligations necessarily go along with rights. Thus justice must include the apportionment of both rights and obligations, advantages and disadvantages, with the criterion for the proper apportionment being the maximization of true freedom.

Order is a condition in which rights and obligations are apportioned in a regular, predictable manner. There can be a *just order*, in which rights and obligations are apportioned in a regular, predictable manner and in such a way that freedom is maximized, or an unjust order, in which rights and obligations are apportioned in a regular, predictable manner, but in such a way that freedom is minimized (or at least falls far short of being maximized). Or there can be *disorder*, in which rights and obligations are apportioned in a capricious, shifting manner, instead of in a regular, predictable manner.

All of the concepts discussed in this section are important to a proper understanding of politics and its role in man's affairs. This detour through the briar patch of concepts will prove very worth while. Armed with these concepts we are now ready to do some careful thinking about the role man's political relationships play in society.

THE ROLE OF POLITICS IN SOCIETY
At the beginning of this chapter I noted a basic paradox:

Man needs man; yet man cannot get along with man. It is out of this tension between social need and estrangement that the role and purpose of politics in human society arises.

Man's Excessive Self-love

The previous chapter carefully noted and sought to document the fact that something tragic has gone wrong with human nature. Instead of man's being marked by a proper balance between love for others and love for one's self, man's self-love has run wild. Man's innate inclination is to be obsessed with himself and, forgetting God, to place himself and his welfare above respect for the integrity and rights of others. Man—sunk in sin—becomes estranged from his fellow man whom he needs, and human society is threatened with disintegration.

The natural tendency of man's inordinate self-love—a tendency which would become actuality unless checked by other forces—is to violate the rights of others by denying his obligations toward others. The murderer assumes that his desire for power, financial rewards or revenge should take precedence over his victim's right to life; the prejudiced person assumes his inordinate pride in his racial, religious or linguistic group should take precedence over the right to just treatment by members of some other racial, religious or linguistic group; and the exploitive employer assumes his greed for money should take precedence over his employees' rights for safety or a fair return for their work. Time and time again man's natural inclination leads him to place his own welfare and pleasures above the rights of others. Discrimination, exploitation and disregard for the integrity of the person are the inevitable fruits.

Thus the excessive self-love found in individuals leads with an inexorable logic to disorder on the societal level, as each man pursues his own welfare in disregard of the rights of others and his obligations toward them. The survival of the fittest—the strongest, the most skillful, the most cunning—becomes the guiding law. Order is lost, for each man acts not on the basis of accepted standards and rules but on the basis of his personal needs and desires. Society, in the sense of persons living and working together in community, becomes impossible.

Disorder such as this of necessity means injustice. Justice, as we have just seen, is the apportionment of rights and obligations in such a way that true freedom—including the freedom to act within groups—is maximized. But for justice to exist, there must be order. If there is no order —no regular, predictable pattern according to which rights and obligations are apportioned—rights and obligations will be apportioned in a random, hit-or-miss fashion, with happenstance combinations of individuals' strength, cunning and conscience determining the apportionment. Chaos, fear, whim, unpredictability will reign. The jungle will replace society. And in a jungle no one is free. When one's rights are not recognized, he is no longer free, but is bound by other individuals and groups over whom he has no control. And when one is not free, his humanity remains broken and truncated; his unique creative capabilities cannot be exercised and developed.

But one might suggest that perhaps persons can be persuaded voluntarily to restrict their actions against others by being shown that if everyone did so an orderly society with true community and personal freedom would result. All we need to do is to convince people it is in their own self-interest to restrain their actions against others. This would lead to the personal freedom we all need and desire.[13] But Mancur Olson's theory of collective action helps show why we cannot realistically expect this to happen. Olson argues, in discussing private organizations, that where collective benefits are at stake, that is, benefits which accrue to all persons whether or not they are members of an organization, it is not rational for the individual to support the organization.

> The individual member of the typical large organization . . . will not have a noticeable effect on the situation of his organization, and he can enjoy any improvements brought about by others whether or not he has worked in support of his organization.[14]

Each person's contribution to the organization is too small to affect it and its ability to achieve its goals. Thus whether or not one supports the organization does not affect the likelihood of his receiving the benefits of the organization. As a consequence the rational thing for the self-interested individual to do is not to support the organization.

The same theory can be applied to the problem of achieving societal order through individual, voluntary action. To achieve order each person must pay a cost in the form of restricting his actions, yet each person's contribution to the achievement of the order is so small that he could fail to restrict his actions without destroying the order. Thus each individual could not pay the costs (not restrict his actions) and yet enjoy the benefits (the freedom accruing from a just order). But the problem is that since this is true for all persons, many—maybe even most— would seek to gain the benefits without paying the costs, thereby destroying the order. One is driven back to the conclusion that some other way to establish a just order is needed.

In summary, the natural results of man's excessive self-love and the logic of individual action lead on the societal level, unless checked by other forces, to a chaotic war of all against all, in which no one is free and no one is able to reach the full essence of humanity.

Society-wide Authority

What rescues man from sliding into a war of all against all and in actuality makes community and true freedom possible is the existence of certain forces which act to restrict and limit man's excessive self-love and its consequences. As noted in chapter 2, Christianity teaches that God works in the hearts and lives of individuals, restraining them from following their natural inclinations into lives marked totally by self-love.[15] Societal institutions such as families, churches, fraternal organizations and informal peer groups also act, through both their formal rules and informal norms of behavior to restrict the trampling of others' rights. Such institutions have the implicit or explicit threat of ostracism and social disgrace, which, in view of man's social nature, gives them a significant sanction with which to encourage obedience to their standards.

Although these factors in and by themselves are insufficient to assure an adequate basis for community, they do help make politics possible. By creating a basis for the sense of legitimacy essential for the political resolution of conflicts, they help create the minimal sense of respect for others and the spirit of forbearance and good will necessary for politics to function.

Politics, in turn, plays an indispensable role in making community possible. Earlier I defined government and politics in terms of their possession of inclusive, society-wide authority. But their authority is not authority for authority's sake. The exercise of authority ought not to be an end in itself. The authority of government is to be directed at the establishment of order out of the chaos with which man's excessive self-love is constantly threatening society. Government, because of the authority and legitimacy it possesses, is able to allocate rights and obligations within a society. It establishes order—a known, predictable pattern of rights and obligations of individuals and groups of individuals.

But the political process does not possess the role of simply creating order for order's sake. Order ought not to be an end in itself any more than the exercise of authority is an end in itself. A certain type of order must be sought. The order government ought to seek is one which maximizes true freedom in society, thereby creating a just order. And, as seen earlier in this chapter, freedom and justice are defined ultimately by man's being given the fullest opportunity to develop and exercise his creative capacity, in keeping with God's law of love, a creative capacity which is reflected in men's group and individual lives. Thus the government, while it cannot force man to be free, while it cannot force man to exercise and develop his creativity, while it cannot force man to act in love, can and should help to assure the widest possible opportunity for man to be free, creative, loving. The government's purpose is to enable man to be as fully as possible the creative, thinking, willing, loving, culture-creating being God destined him to be.

This is the conclusion to which the concepts of man, society and politics discussed earlier drive us. Man is made in the likeness of God himself, destined for a life of creative love lived in community with his fellow man. Yet man's sin—his excessive self-love—threatens all mankind with a breakdown of community and thereby with the suffocating of the creative life. It is impossible to create the just order needed for the reestablishment of community and for the possibility of the creative life through physical, violent coercion or through personal, nonviolent coercive pressures. Thus politics—the political resolution of conflicts—remains as man's only hope for the establishment of a just order.

One is thereby driven, if he accepts the Christian concepts of man and society presented in chapter 2, to this conclusion: *The purpose of politics is to establish an order which maximizes man's true freedom, that is, man's opportunity to develop and exercise his creative capacities in keeping with God's law of love.* It can be stated simply, but many concepts and insights underlie it and countless implications and applications extend from it.

Figure 1 summarizes the basic concepts underlying this conception of the role of politics in society. Man is the starting point. He is a social being, destined to live a rich, meaningful life of freedom and creative love in community with his fellow man. The problem is that man's own excessive self-love disrupts the society on which his free, creative life depends. The staircase back to the possibility of a creative life and the potential fulfilling of his destiny leads first to the remnants of goodness preserved in man and to human institutions such as the family, church and peer group. The sense of forbearance and respect they nurture make the next step—politics—possible. Through the political process a just order can be established, one in which rights and obligations are so apportioned that true freedom is maximized. This just order then once again makes community (man's living together in harmony) possible. And that community makes the creative life possible for man. Thus an individual does not end up as the perfectly loving, creative being he was intended to be, but, in spite of being surrounded by other men dominated by self-love who constantly threaten his freedom and thereby his ability to live a free, creative life, he does have the opportunity to develop and exercise his creative capacities. In that sense, he is free.

Two additional observations are needed. The first relates to the fact that sometimes an argument has arisen between those who advocate that the proper role of politics is only to maintain order and establish justice and those who think politics should play a broader role in

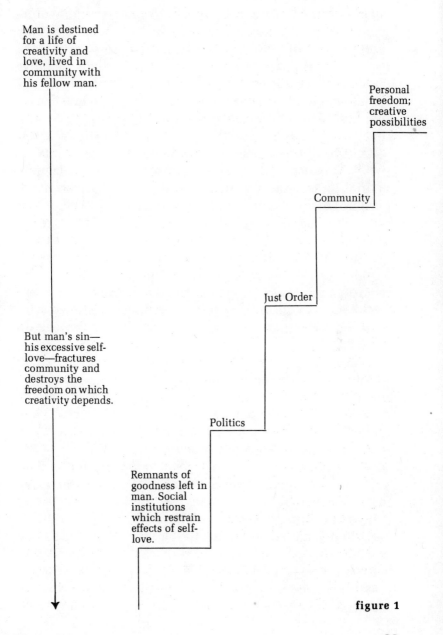

Man is destined for a life of creativity and love, lived in community with his fellow man.

Personal freedom; creative possibilities

Community

Just Order

But man's sin—his excessive self-love—fractures community and destroys the freedom on which creativity depends.

Politics

Remnants of goodness left in man. Social institutions which restrain effects of self-love.

figure 1

63

society.[16] The latter argue that politics has a general obligation to seek to correct wrongs and to show love and mercy to all of suffering humanity. Those who are acquainted with this controversy may conclude that the above position supports a severely limited role of politics in human affairs. Justice and order, and not general Christian love and mercy, are stressed. But when one recalls that human freedom, and thereby order and justice as well, are not only threatened by certain criminal elements in society but also by a wide variety of economic, social and natural forces and organizations, the role of government becomes great. It has the lofty role of carving a just order, with the resulting freedom, out of the chaos of hate, greed, violence and disregard for others into which man's excessive self-love has led him. The tragic history of workers exploited by employers, racial minorities suppressed by majority groups, consumers bilked by unscrupulous businessmen, gives testimony to where man's excessive self-love leads when government's regulative role is weak or missing.

Yet the role of the government is also limited. What must be remembered is that for every right or advantage the government imposes in its search for a just order it must also impose additional obligations. And each added obligation restricts man's freedom of action—the very thing the government is supposed to expand. Thus the political process should be a delicate weighing and balancing process in which there is a constant search for the maximization of true human freedom. Sometimes, of course, the proper response will be fairly obvious, as in the earlier cited case of weighing the right of women to safety from sexual assaults versus the right of potential rapists to act out their sexual violence. But other cases are not so clear. Is the advantage of assuring ill persons adequate medical care without devastating bills through some form of government health insurance worth the imposition of the necessary disadvantages on hospitals, doctors and private insurance companies? The answer is not immediately clear. Even persons who agree that the proper test should be the maximization of true freedom will be found in disagreement. The role of politics being advocated here establishes a clear criterion by which to evaluate the propriety of governmental programs, but the application of that criterion to specific issues does not necessarily result in clear-cut answers.[17] A delicate weighing, balancing process is involved.

A second observation is that the purpose of government and politics for which I have argued does not lead to government's playing the role of a moral busybody, prying into everyone's business and seeking to force everyone to live creative, loving lives. The emphasis is on freedom, not on futile attempts to force persons to be creative and loving. Government should maximize true freedom, not force even the loftiest of moral standards onto anyone. True freedom is here defined in terms of maximizing the opportunity for living creative lives in keeping with God's law of love. Attaining this sort of freedom necessitates imposing obligations on others. Therefore, acts of persons which would be destructive of others' opportunities to act creatively in love must be thwarted by government action, but the goal and criterion is freedom of opportunity—not the use of government to impose my or anyone's code of ethics onto others.

The Imperfection of Politics
The previous section stressed the crucial and lofty role politics plays in human society. Yet another paradox remains. Although the role is lofty, the performance is often shoddy. Somehow it seems that politics, instead of operating on the assigned heights of justice, order, freedom and

creative opportunities for all men, in practice is frequently found wallowing in the mire of compromise, broken promises and special-interest favors. The gap between promise and performance can largely be explained by four factors. It is these factors which underlie the imperfection of politics.

The Unbroken Circle of Self-love. Politics, as just described, is basically a solution to the problems resulting from man's sin, but the difficulty with this solution is that the root cause of the problems is inherent in the solution. Since all men are marked by an excessive self-love, the men who constitute and run the government are as marked by this and are as subject to its corruptive influence as are the men they are regulating. Their vision is distorted, their goals often self-serving and their prejudices intact.

Politics thereby is a case of a physician seeking to cure an infection by a means which is itself contaminated by the same infection. Politics is infected by the same problem whose effects it is supposed to remedy! In the process the cure sometimes becomes worse than the disease. At best, the cure is going to remain incomplete, imperfect. As a result one frequently finds governmental programs which are aimed more at enriching a few powerful interests than at creating wide economic opportunity for the many and governmental regulations which are turned into means to limit competition instead of protecting the consumer. The Watergate scandal of the Nixon Administration was unique in the extent to which high officials were acting illegally and were seeking to conceal criminal acts, but the specter of individuals using their position of power more for private gain than for maximizing the creative opportunities in society was not unique.

What then happens to the role of government in society? Is there any basis on which to expect government to be able to play, even imperfectly, the role in society outlined above? There is. First, there is evidence that politics—at least in the United States—attracts men and women somewhat more altruistic, somewhat more dedicated to the welfare of others and somewhat more knowledgeable than is the general populace. Several studies have shown that political leaders are more committed to the protection of civil liberties and other principles of democratic government than is the mass of the citizenry.[18] Another study showed that persons who had selected themselves as potential public officeholders were more knowledgeable about public affairs and more committed to civil liberties than persons who did not see themselves as potential officeholders.[19] One study found high-level American bureaucrats making such statements as these about their public obligations:

I have a feeling of participation in something important and worthwhile.

These are significant days, I have a feeling of participating in them—of working on world problems.

I don't feel I would be doing something of importance if I were to work for industry. They are not interested in the public welfare.

Who could possibly be interested in selling soap?[20] Admittedly, little research has been done on what motivates persons to become politically active and many possible motives exist—financial gain, power, prestige, as well as an opportunity to serve altruistically. But given the long hours, insecurity of tenure and frequent public malignment which goes along with political leadership, and given the opportunities to attain power, financial gain and prestige outside politics in safer, more secure atmospheres, it is reasonable to conclude that altruism probably plays an important role in many persons' attraction to political careers. The hazards are too great and the rewards too uncertain to explain it otherwise. One congressman, when asked what motivates congressmen to run for Congress, put it this way:

> Money is not the explanation because many, if not most, congressmen could earn a larger income in other fields. A desire for security is certainly not the answer since there is little security for a congressman who must run for re-election every two years. Certainly it is not the working conditions. Most members work far longer hours than they would be forced to put in were they in business. . . .
>
> What is it which attracts a man to this type of life? Some would say it is the desire for power. Some the desire for prestige. Both are partial answers, but they do not present a full explanation. The chief interest in holding a congressional office lies in the satisfaction one can gain from feeling he is actively participating in the important decisions of government. . . .
>
> Thus the fascination of congress lies in the nature of the office and the real opportunities it offers the incumbent to contribute to the welfare of the American people.[21]

A basis, in fact, exists for concluding that there is a tendency for political leaders to be able to rise above self-interest and the distraction of self-love to a somewhat greater degree than is true of the general public. Yet the point ought not to be overemphasized. The increase in altruism is only marginal and, of course, is not true at all for many in positions of political leadership.

A second factor increasing the likelihood that a government completely composed of imperfect men can still play a positive role in society are the norms and expectations society holds for political officials, combined with the ever-present possibility of publicity and exposure. Society expects political officials to possess a certain public spiritedness, to be concerned for the general welfare, to be truthful in their dealings and to be faithful to the Constitution and laws. Deviations from these norms and expectations—when exposed—are likely to lead to public humiliation and disgrace. Officials forced out of high office because of misconduct, such as Alger Hiss, Sherman Adams, H. Robert Haldeman, John Ehrlichman, Spiro Agnew and Richard Nixon, are rather pathetic figures. Their careers are ruined. Persons pursuing more private careers do not risk the same exposure and the same disgrace and dishonor as do political officials. Thus the pressure on political officials to take the broad public interest into account and, at the least, to avoid outright corruption and special-interest pleading is greater than it is for most of us in our more private lives.

A third factor explaining the ability of government to play a freedom-creating role in society in spite of the excessive self-love of governmental officials is the open, regularized processes of government. Governmental decision-makers operate openly and through known, established procedures. Thus checks are present which are not present when decisions are made privately and capriciously. In a lawless society I would never know what my neighbor was going to do next and thus I would have no way to thwart the acts which would be detrimental to the freedom of myself and others. But, because government operates openly and according to known, established rules, I know what governmental actions are going to be taken and can seek to support or change those actions. Greater justice, greater personal freedom, is likely to result under such circumstances than under the personal whims of countless individuals.

In summary, there is a basis on which to believe that even though political officials are limited and corrupted by the same problem of excessive self-love which bedevils all mankind, politics can still fulfill its role in society to a significant degree. Nevertheless, the continuing problem of sinful men running government assures us that government will remain an imperfect means of seeking a just order; it will remain an instrument prone to failings and errors, and therefore will deserve a certain suspicion and skepticism.

Incomplete Knowledge. Also causing the imperfection of politics is the incomplete knowledge on which political leaders usually must rest their decisions. Even morally perfect political leaders who desire to so balance rights and obligations that true freedom is maximized often err because of their ignorance and misinformation and strike balances which would not maximize freedom. To judge accurately which policy alternatives will maximize freedom requires a completeness of knowledge that is beyond man's grasp. Typically the facts are in dispute, consequences uncertain, possible alternatives not even discovered and tangled threads unravelable. That policies in such circumstances are often imperfect and result in injustices for segments of the population is hardly a wonder.

Compromise. In politics conflict is the norm. Especially given the incomplete knowledge and the morally imperfect nature of the political decision-makers, it is difficult to reach resolutions of these conflicts based on rational standards. Instead, compromise—at least in democratic regimes—is the normal means of reaching agreement. Individuals representing differing points of view and differing power blocs negotiate and bargain until they reach an agreement all sides can accept. Most political battles are not fought in the lofty realm of ideals and beliefs but down in the grubby world of power and compromise. The end result is imperfection.

Time. Politics is also a time-consuming process. Because of the formal decision-making steps and the compromises and adjustments often involved, it is a slow means to achieve change. Progress usually is better measured in decades than in months. This is disheartening to those impatient for change, but this slowness is inherent in politics' very nature, in its compromising, negotiating, persuading, legitimacy-building character. Again politics is less than perfect; injustices and exploitation last for years as the wheels of politics slowly move.

The final picture of politics which emerges is that of an indispensable process—indispensable if man is to live in community and even partially achieve the destiny of freedom and creativity for which he is made—yet an imperfect, even sordid, process. One is reminded of Winston Churchill's famous statement that democracy is the worst form of government—except for all the others. One can say that politics is the worst way to settle disputes and build community—except for all the others. The basic alternative to politics is violence, which can only lead back to the jungle where no one is free and thus where no one can attain his full humanity.

It is out of the concepts of man, society and politics presented in this chapter and the previous one that my critique of current American public policies and of where present-day leaders are seeking to take us emerges. Most of our political leaders misread man, therefore misread the ills of American society and therefore prescribe the wrong medicine. It is only by returning to the basics, to the fundamental building block of society, man himself, that one can start on the right road to a better society and a better political order. Thus the concepts and distinctions made in these chapters are essential to a knowing critique of the political world. Armed with these concepts and distinctions, we can now turn directly to that troubled, uncertain arena.

Politics in
American Society

II

4
From Burke to Marcuse: Domestic Political Options

THE POLITICS OF A POST-CHRISTIAN WORLD has given us Vietnam, Watergate, urban decay, black ghettoes, suffocating pollution and the threat of nuclear devastation. A basic thesis of this book is that the political alternatives being offered Americans today are morally and practically bankrupt. Their presuppositions are false, their diagnoses misleading and their prescriptions disastrous.

But can the values and insights of evangelical Christianity lead to a politics any less marked by violence, militarism, hate, materialism and corruption than do the values and insights of naturalism, scientism, positivism and existentialism? I believe they can. They at least offer us a basis for understanding the nature and source of our problems and why past approaches have failed to create a just, humane politics. Parts II and III apply the insights and concepts developed in part I to the ongoing political world, thereby developing a critique of past and present approache$ and the outlines of a new way. Part II concentrates on the world of American politics and domestic policy concerns; part III on the world of international politics and foreign policy concerns.

My interest is not as much with specific policy issues and controversies as it is with the combinations of assumptions, points of view and perspectives with which one approaches the more specific issues and problems to which policy formation must address itself. The primary focus is on the United States, but much of what I write applies equally well to the other modern, liberal-democratic societies of western Europe, North America and Australasia.

This chapter is concerned with the basic approaches which underlie and inform current domestic policies being pursued by the American government and why they have not been serving us well. The next chapter seeks to develop a better way—one self-consciously based on Christian insights and values.

THREE TRADITIONAL APPROACHES
Traditionally, there have been three fundamental perspectives which have guided man's approach to the forging of domestic policies. All three have played important roles in American political history; all three continue to mold the perspectives with which we view policy choices. It is impossible, in the space available here, to analyze fully these three basic perspectives and to note all of their distinctive variations. Yet an understanding of their broad outlines is useful in understanding the current malaise and failures of American politics. It is therefore to these three traditionally held approaches to policy making that we turn first.

Traditional Conservatism
Traditional conservatism received its clearest and most in-

fluential defense from Edmund Burke (1729-1797).[1] Burke and his followers started with the basic premise that man, while capable of goodness and progress, is limited by his natural frailties and tendencies toward evil. Conservatism's view of man, while not one of unrelieved pessimism, did stress man's weaknesses. Whatever progress man has made toward civility and mutual respect is constantly threatening to regress into hostility and hate.

A second basic premise of traditional conservatism was the organic nature of human society. The conservatives saw society as intimately bound up with both the past and the future. Present society is only one link in a never-ending chain leading from past generations to the present generation to future generations. Each generation is what it is because of the achievements or failures, progress or decay, of past generations, and each generation contributes to future generations through its own achievements or failures, progress or decay.

From these two basic premises the conservatives' view of government and politics emerged. Because of man's weaknesses, man's attempts to recreate society by his reason and will are doomed to failure; because of the organic nature of society, experience and the accumulated wisdom of past generations reflected in existing institutions are dependable guides to progress. Thus when men, inspired by an abstract concept of the good society, seek to use government to create that society, their failure is foreordained. For man's will and reason are too fallible and the real world too complex to be subjected to this sort of simple manipulation. Rather, what is needed is to build upon the accumulated experience of past generations, seeking improvements and modifications, but always guided by experience—not by lofty, abstract schemes.

Sometimes conservatism is pictured as simply opposing all change and as favoring very weak or limited government. But this was not true of traditional, Burkean conservatism. In fact, the conservative's mistrust of man and recognition of his frailties led him to accept a fairly strong government. A strong government is needed to restrain and guide man. René Williamson rightly points out that such conservatives as Bismarck in imperial Germany and Alexander Hamilton in the American constitutional convention worked for strong governments which could work to achieve the common good (as they defined it).[2] Nor was Burkean conservatism simply anti-change, pro-status quo. As a tree grows and develops, so also the conservative saw the need for government to develop and change. Radical, abrupt change informed by man's reason and will is what the conservative feared, not gradual change based on man's experiences. Burke once wrote,

> Our political system is placed in a just correspondence and symmetry with the order of the world, wherein . . . moulding together the great mysterious incorporation of the human race, the whole, at one time is never old, or middle-aged, or young, but . . . moves on through the varied tenor of perpetual decay, fall, renovation, and progression. Thus, by preserving the method of nature in the conduct of the State, in what we improve, we are never wholly new; in what we retain, we are never wholly obsolete.[3]

In many respects the conservative view of man and society comes close to the Christian view. Both recognize man's limitations and evil, as well as his potentialities and virtues; both recognize the inherent complexity of man and society, rejecting attempts to reduce man to a single dimension.

Yet conservatism fails in its refusal to recognize any norm or standard outside of man or society by which man is to order his affairs. God has warned us: "Do not be conformed to this world but be transformed by the renewal of your mind, that you may prove what is the will of God, what is good and acceptable and perfect.''[4] But the traditional conservative, instead of ordering his affairs by the will of God, follows the experience and wisdom (or lack of wisdom) of an actual, ongoing society. Whether that society is at a comparatively high or low level of morality and justice there is no way to evaluate and break out of that level. The past becomes a prison—and the conservative has thrown away the key. What was and what is, rather than a standard outside any particular political system, becomes the norm. Conservatism's taking experience embodied in current institutions and practices as being normative surely is a prime example of being conformed to the world.

A Christian finds in the will of God a standard which enables him to judge any particular society. In chapter 3 I showed how Christian values and insights conceive the proper role of politics as the maximizing of true freedom through the creation of a just order. Not that the answers to society's problems will always be clear. In fact, sometimes they will not be clear at all! But the standards of order, justice, freedom and opportunities for a creative life I discussed earlier at least offer a basis for evaluating and judging which the traditional conservative does not have.

Professor Williamson has stated the central problem with conservatism well:

However, when one looks more closely at the conservative's belief in institutions, it sometimes turns out that his belief is a form of defeatism. In such cases institutions are a refuge against the attempt of people to create better ones. The conservative then believes in the American way of life by default. In the absence of objective external standards, which he feels do not exist or cannot be known, he falls back on what he has.[5]

79

Classical Liberalism

Classical liberalism is a second thread which has heavily influenced modern man's attitudes toward political policies. It received its clearest and most influential articulation by thinkers such as John Locke (1632-1704), Adam Smith (1723-1790), and, in the United States, Thomas Jefferson (1743-1826).

Classical liberalism started with the basic assumption of the goodness and rationality of man.[6] Man is good; it is society and human institutions which corrupt him. Man is rational; it is ignorance which interferes with his making wise, reasonable choices. A second basic assumption was the complete autonomy of the individual. Professor George Sabine described the individualism of seventeenth-century liberalism this way: "Not man as a priest or a soldier, as the member of a guild or an estate, but man as a bare human being, a 'masterless man,' appeared to be the solid fact."[7] Individual man was seen as the key unit of society; it was individual man whose rights must be protected and freedoms safeguarded.

These first two assumptions of liberalism led to a third: Individual good and collective good are indistinguishable. Believing in the natural goodness and rationality of man, and convinced of the supreme worth of the individual, it was easy for the liberals to conclude that what was good for the individual was good for society. Safeguarding the freedom of the good, rational individual would lead to the good society. In commenting on Locke's thought Sabine expressed it this way: "Like later liberals he assumed that the two things—preservation of the common good and protection of private rights—come to the same thing."[8]

These three basic assumptions of classical liberalism led quite naturally to a view of politics which called for government with a very limited role in society. In many respects liberalism was a reaction to the mercantilism and political authoritarianism of the seventeenth century. The mercantilist economic policies of seventeenth-century governments created monopolies, subsidized businesses and in many other ways extended government into economic issues. In the process a rigid, stultifying hierarchy of privilege was created. Liberalism was also a reaction to the political authoritarianism of many of the emerging national states which suppressed individual rights and freedoms. The government was the basic threat to individual freedom, through both its mercantilist economic policies and its authoritarian rule. Freedom was therefore defined largely in negative terms as the absence of governmental restraints. To the liberal mind, if man's goodness and rationality were to bear fruit, if the worth of the individual was to be recognized, and if thereby the collective good was to be attained, then the individual should be freed from the restrictive, oppressive regulations of government. "That government which governs least, governs best," epitomizes the liberals' faith.

The most basic error of liberalism lay in its assumption of the essential goodness of man—an assumption which led it to a negative view of freedom which was entirely too narrow. Believing man to be good, yet observing evil everywhere in society, the liberals latched onto the mercantilist, authoritarian governments of the day as the source of evil. Thus the conclusion logically followed that if government could only be severely limited human freedom would flower. What the liberals' presuppositions blinded them to was the continuing need of strong government to curb the evil propensities within man himself. Thus when liberalism largely triumphed in the eighteenth and early nineteenth centuries—when combined with the industrial revolution—it led to a situation where private employers shamelessly exploited workers, requiring even ten-year-old children to work over eighty hours a week under dangerous, unhealthy conditions,[9] and where monopolistic companies abused their competitors and consumers alike. Private wealth and unrestrained capitalism proved to be as capable of destroying personal freedom as had government.

Liberalism did help unleash vast economic growth and expansion, and it did, in time, lead to political recognition and protection of basic individual rights and civil liberties, but its naivete concerning the nature of man led it to underestimate grievously the evils man would be willing to wreak upon his fellow man in pursuit of his own self-interest. That the common good would naturally arise from each individual's pursuit of his own good simply was not true. Individual man proved to be too sinful, too dominated by self-love. And the "invisible hand" or social law which would guarantee that the individual pursuit of self-interest would lead to the common good proved nonexistent. It was only when governments started to assert their regulative powers that the status of industrial workers was raised and the worst features of monopolistic practices eliminated.

Revisionist Liberalism and Democratic Socialism

In the nineteenth century, the exploitation of industrial workers by large-scale industries and the attendant social ills posed problems which neither traditional conservatism nor classical liberalism could solve. Conservatives lacked the standards by which to condemn the grievous social problems or to prescribe remedies. Classical liberalism, based on very limited government and a narrow, negative definition of freedom, was unable to recognize the loss of freedom suffered by the workers and their families for what it was and unable to recommend a remedy.

Into this void stepped a number of thinkers who, while retaining some of the basic assumptions of classical liberalism, turned it around, favoring strong government intervention in society's economic and social relations.[10] These revisionist liberals, led initially by John Stuart Mill (1806-1893), who, as John Hallowell put it, "laid the foundations for socialism while claiming to uphold the principles of Classical economics,"[11] and later by Thomas Hill Green (1836-1882) and the Fabian Socialists, fundamentally revised classical liberalism. The end product was state welfarism and democratic socialism.

Hallowell has summarized the similarities between classical liberalism and democratic socialism:

Both liberalism and socialism start from a belief in the autonomy of human reason and in the perfectibility of man. Both assign redemptive powers to Nature or to History. Both have as their goal the freeing of the individual from arbitrary and capricious authority.[12]

Revisionist liberalism retained the optimistic view of man held by classical liberalism and continued to see man as an autonomous individual.

The chief difference was that while classical liberalism saw government and its regulations as the chief—perhaps even the only—threat to personal freedom and therefore defined freedom chiefly in terms of the absence of government interference, the revisionist liberals saw that freedom could be restricted equally effectively by nongovernmental forces.

Green, according to Sabine, argued that

The freedom of an Irish tenant to contract with the owner of his land becomes a mere formality when eviction means starvation. In such cases the actual coercion which an employer or a landlord can exert under the legal form of a contract is in fact . . . far more oppressive and far more destructive of effective freedom than the legal coercion exerted by the state when it abridges the right of contract to protect the weaker party.[13]

83

Thus Green argued for a strong, active government which would interfere with existing economic and social relations in order to assure that the actual opportunity for acting out a rich, full life would be guaranteed. On this basis he argued for public health measures, legislation limiting the hours of work, compulsory education and more.[14]

From the thought of Green and other revisionist liberals it was a small step to democratic socialism.[15] Non-Marxist, democratic socialism does not rest on a theory of class conflict or teach revolutionary, violent change, and thus it is really an extension of revisionist liberalism. It urges even more government activity to equalize the opportunities for all individuals to develop their potentials and to exercise their wills.

In many respects the concept of freedom the revisionist liberals developed is very close to the concept of freedom I believe a Christian understanding of society and man directs. The concept of true freedom developed in chapter 3 is more than a mere absence of political restraints, but takes into account the entire political, societal and natural context within which each of us lives. In this respect revisionist liberalism was a marked advance over classical liberalism and recognized a fact that had become increasingly evident as society had become increasingly interdependent.

But where revisionist liberalism went wrong was in its continued assumption of the goodness of man. Just as the classical liberals erred in locating the source of evil in political restraints, so the revisionist liberals erred in locating the source of evil in economic relations. Thus, just as classical liberals put too much faith in the free, autonomous individual, revisionist liberals put too much faith in government regulation and control. They usually did not recognize the imperfections of politics I discussed earlier. They did not give sufficient weight to the moral im-

perfections and the limited knowledge of political officials. They thereby underestimated the intractableness of
the inequities and evils they sought to eradicate and over-
estimated the extent to which political action could eradicate social and economic problems.

THREE CURRENT APPROACHES

The three traditional approaches which have historically
guided man's reaction to the political world are not highly
abstract theories, forged in insulated ivory towers. Rather,
they were forged in the heat of political battle and refined
in the fire of political combat. The course of each one's
history has been in the political arena of swirling events,
clashing wills and—frequently—pragmatic compromises.

Thus in practice traditional conservatism, classical liberalism and revisionist liberalism have not been held in
pure and undiluted form. More typically in the press of
political combat, their opponents have caricatured them
and their proponents have compromised them. The final
result is a confusing array of alternative perspectives and
approaches to the task of policy formation, perspectives
and approaches which include various aspects of one or
more of the three traditional approaches. But within this
array three generally definable alternatives can be located
in the United States today: conservatism, liberalism and
new left radicalism. These are the three alternative combinations of assumptions, points of view and perspectives
which have led—and misled—our age. This section of the
chapter sorts out these three alternatives and shows how
they have contributed to our current political malaise.

Conservatism

American Conservatism and Classical Liberalism. To a
large degree conservatism, as the term is used in the
United States, is a misnomer. American conservatism is

closer to classical liberalism than to traditional conservatism. Once this truth is grasped much about American politics is clarified.

Senator Barry Goldwater, the Republicans' 1964 presidential candidate, is still acknowledged as one of the leading spokesmen for the Republican party's conservative wing. His 1960 best-selling book, *The Conscience of a Conservative,* is almost pure classical liberalism. Government is seen as the prime enemy of freedom: "Throughout history, government has proved to be the chief instrument for thwarting man's liberty."[16] Goldwater goes on to prescribe the classical liberal medicine: severely limited government. He defines the legitimate function of government as limited to maintaining internal order, keeping foreign foes at bay, administering justice, removing obstacles to the free interchange of goods—the exercise of these powers makes it possible for men to follow their chosen pursuits with maximum freedom.[17]

Elements of traditional conservatism do occasionally creep into Goldwater's thought, especially at one point where he warns against those who would "harness the society's political and economic forces into a collective effort to *compel* 'progress.' In this approach, I believe they fight against Nature."[18] In the same vein, he also speaks approvingly of learning from the accumulated wisdom of history,[19] but what that accumulated wisdom seems to tell him is that a classical liberal view of government and society is needed.

Thus Goldwater ends up calling for a radical program of change—one that would repeal current farm programs, vastly alter labor-management relations and do away with most welfare programs. He would remake the American political landscape, guided by the basic tenets of classical liberalism.

Although Goldwater is one of the most conservative

American political leaders, his point of view, including his commitment to the tenets of classical liberalism, is supported by many other conservative spokesmen. In his first inaugural address Richard Nixon gave vent to a classical liberal view of man:

> To a crisis of the spirit we need an answer of the spirit. And to find that answer we need only look within ourselves.
>
> When we listen to "the better angels of our nature," we find that they celebrate the simple things, the basic things, such as goodness, decency, and love, kindness.[20]

Later, he went on to say, "I know America. I know the heart of America is good."[21] Although Nixon avoided fully embracing the classical liberal optimistic view of man, he clearly saw man as predominantly good. Given this belief, Nixon's frequent stress on and confidence in private and local initiative in meeting social problems becomes understandable. However, he was enough of a political pragmatist—and perhaps enough of a traditional conservative—that he never sought to reduce governmental regulative power in the way Goldwater and other more conservative leaders have.

Political commentator William F. Buckley, Jr. expressed a more purely classical liberal position when he wrote, "It isn't only that the Executive must relinquish power to Congress. Both should relinquish power to—if the expression is not profane—the people."[22]

The conservative wing of the Democratic party also exhibits the impact of classical liberal thought. Senator Sam Ervin of North Carolina once said, "One condition of freedom is as much absence of regimentation of the individual as possible. The stronger the government is, the less freedom the individual has."[23]

American Conservatism and Traditional Conservatism. Although one does not have to read long in the speeches and writings of American conservative political leaders to find numerous examples of classical liberal assumptions and conclusions, one must search long and hard for examples of traditional conservative assumptions and conclusions. The simple honesty and goodness of the free individual is celebrated, but not his weaknesses and frailties; the autonomy of the individual is stressed, but not the organic nature of society; the need to limit national government power is preached, but not the need to maintain continuity with past policies.

Nevertheless, a paradox emerges: Most American conservatives, while in their public statements extolling the classical liberal view of government and ignoring the traditional conservative view, often act more like traditional conservatives than classical liberals. Programs of social and economic intervention, even though normally opposed by conservatives while in the process of enactment, are rarely made objects of repeal attempts once enacted. Social security, farm price supports, Medicare and Medicaid, and various civil rights acts are all examples. President Nixon used deficit spending and wage and price controls—measures long opposed by conservatives—after their use by liberals for many years had made them acceptable. Nixon's attempts to dismantle many of President Johnson's War on Poverty programs stand as almost the only example in the twentieth century of a conservative government's attempting to repeal programs earlier enacted over conservative objections. The typical pattern has been for American conservatives, when they hold political power, to make modifications and refinements in existing programs, but not to make major changes in them (either through repeal or expansions). The voice is the voice of classical liberalism, but the hand is the hand of traditional conservatism. American conservatism's ideological commitment is to classical liberalism, yet it is sufficiently pragmatic to be normally willing to settle for the actions of traditional conservatism.

American Conservatism: An Evaluation. American conservatism is clearly not the answer to the problems and disorientations of today's society. In fact, it is a major cause of them. To the extent American conservatism holds to the classical liberal ideal of weak government, it holds to an archaic ideal that may have been relevant to the eighteenth-century's mercantilist, authoritarian governments and largely agricultural societies, but is totally inappropriate to the twentieth-century's liberal-democratic governments and interdependent, industrialized societies. To the extent American conservatism practices a traditional conservatism, it seeks to approach complex problems with no guiding standard. As a result inertia and special interests tend to take over.

Concerning the classical liberal strain in American conservatism, Senator Sam Ervin was wrong when he said, "The stronger the government is, the less freedom the individual has." Such a statement is based on the clearly fallacious assumption that only the government limits our freedom. As seen in chapter 3, everyone's freedom of choice is constantly being fenced in by a number of forces.[24] The black who is told he is a free man because the government places no arbitrary restrictions on what he can do or how far he can rise in society is really not free at all if the only school he can attend is an educational nightmare with overcrowded classrooms and incompetent teachers, if he is unable to buy a house outside the ghetto because of tacit agreements among realtors and if he is denied employment because of union and employer discriminatory practices. In fact, he is not any more free than he would be if government legislated that he could not receive a good education or buy a house outside the ghetto or hold other than certain menial jobs. In either case his freedom of action is denied him by forces over which he has no control, and part of the creative opportunities God intended for all men is lost.

Or, to take another example, say an employer of one hundred men in a small shop believes he should pay his workers a decent, living wage. But he is in competition with other shops, whose owners have no desire to pay their workers adequate wages. Instead these owners pay their workers as little as possible, thereby enabling themselves to charge lower prices than the conscientious employer. If the latter were to pay his workers a decent wage, he would have to price his products higher than his competitors, which, in turn, would drive him out of business. Thus he desires to pay his workers decent wages and feels an obligation to do so, yet the free market system says he must either pay his workers inadequate wages or go out of business. Surely his freedom is being limited.

The examples could, of course, be multiplied indefinitely. Time and time again, even in the absence of government regulation—or, better, because of the absence of government regulation—the actions of other individuals or groups limit our freedom of choice. To allow these other restraints on personal freedom to run wild while concerning oneself only with restraints on freedom which originate in government is indefensible. In either case man's freedom, his ability to exercise and develop his God-given creative capacities, is being thwarted, and government is not fulfilling its proper role in society.

To believe that weak government will lead to a just society in which freedom will abound as each person respects his fellow man and seeks to live with him in harmony is to assume a goodness and perfectibility in man that neither experience nor Christianity supports. Weak government is one of the biggest enemies of freedom. Weak government has allowed discrimination against black

Americans to continue for one hundred years after the Civil War; weak government allowed the terrible exploitation of men, women and children in the mines and shops of the nineteenth and early twentieth centuries; weak government permits the pollution of the environment to satisfy private greed; and weak government allows unsafe conditions in American coal mines which kill hundreds of miners each year.[25]

In addition, a conservative who argues for weak government, and thereby implicitly argues for solving societal problems through private, voluntary action, fails to recognize the point made in the prior chapter that an individual rationally pursuing his self-interest will not restrict his actions for the common good.[26] Man does not have to be especially perverse or greedy to render nonpolitical routes to societal betterment impotent. He only has to do what is most convenient or profitable for him personally. It is not rational, for example, for any single individual to contribute to solving the air pollution problem by driving his automobile less, since the lessening of air pollution that would result would be infinitesimal. His driving less would not noticeably improve the quality of the air he breathes, yet it would cause him inconvenience. Only strong government action, which would reduce automobile use on a community-wide basis, can meet the problem.

I must add, however, that if weak government is one of the biggest enemies of freedom, overly strong government is another. The conservative errs not in fearing big, strong government, but in his uncritical opposition to the expansion of government. In order to defend true freedom and the creative opportunities for man which flow from freedom, sometimes government should be expanded, sometimes contracted. But the conservative, lacking a basis on which to judge when government is and is not needed, tends to oppose any and all expansion of governmental power.

In light of these very real shortcomings of American conservatism it is somewhat puzzling to note that there is a tendency for evangelical Christians to support American conservatism.[27] The support evangelicals have given American conservatism seems to rest, first, on the notion that conservatism provides an individualism which is highly compatible with Christianity's conception of the dignity and worth of the individual. Kenneth Elzinga has written about the free market system which

> permits great freedom—freedom in a Christian sense. In common parlance, freedom means self-determination. What I mean is freedom from the power of sin, being freed to do God's will, to do one's God-given calling. The market does not dictate how one is to use private property; consequently the Christian is free to use and consume his or her property, exchange it, share it, or bequeath it, however God directs.[28]

Government intervention, on the other hand—so the argument goes—limits man's freedom of choice, thereby denying him some exercise of the free moral will with which he is endowed by God.

A second basis on which evangelical Christianity is sometimes seen as naturally and properly supportive of American conservatism is the belief that the only way to change society is to change the hearts of individuals. Engaging in political action does not help. The logic underlying this position is that at heart the cause of the social ills which bedevil mankind lies within man himself; man's corrupted nature is the core problem. Thus the way to get at the root cause of social evils is to change the hearts and lives of individual men through the preaching of the gospel. Government by its very nature is limited to dealing with surface manifestations of evil; it cannot get at the root cause. The conclusion seems inescapable that government should limit itself to providing for basic order in society and that individual Christians should seek to correct social and economic ills through their example and personal moral impact on society.

For both these reasons—the desire to protect man's God-given individual freedom and worth, and the possibility of changing society only through changed hearts—evangelical Christianity has often appeared in league with American conservatism, urging limited government and fighting against new political, social and economic programs.

But there are problems with both these reasons for bringing Christianity into alliance with American conservatism. The first reason rests on the old discredited assumption of classical liberalism that only political authorities infringe on one's freedoms. In the statement quoted earlier, for example, Elzinga claims that under the free market system a "Christian is free to use and consume his or her property, exchange it, share it, or bequeath it, however God directs." But is he? What about the black who has the financial means to buy a new house but is prevented from doing so by discriminatory practices of realtors and homeowners, and by a government with no open-housing law? Or remember the example of an employer who wanted to pay his workers a decent, living wage, but whom the market system prevented from so doing on pain of being put out of business. To maximize true personal freedom, thereby freeing man to exercise fully his God-given creative capacity as a man, requires limited, yet active government, not the simple suppression of government.

The position that society can only be truly improved by changing the hearts of individuals and not by government programs contains both truth and error. The truth is in the accurate observation that the best way to get at the root cause of social ills is to change the hearts of mankind and that barring such change what can be accomplished by government is limited. The error lies in the fact that this truth does not support the conclusion that societal ills will be improved more quickly through preaching than politics. This conclusion does not follow for three reasons.

First, not all men—nor even most men—are morally, inwardly good (even in a relative sense). Neither history nor the Bible offers a basis for believing that some day soon most men will change. To some degree the position I am arguing against denies the pervasive, deep-seated nature of sin. Certainly Christ can and does change lives, but Christ himself taught that Christians will always be a minority in the world,[29] and even Christians are often blind to their continuing sins. Thus to expect genuine solutions to widespread social problems through individual regeneration and change is simply not realistic, nor especially biblical.

A second basic error in this approach lies in the fact that often social, economic and political systems prevent even good men from doing much of the good they wish to do. We can go back to the example of the employer who wished to pay his employees decent wages but was pressured by the market system to do otherwise. In addition, government regulations will sometimes block one's efforts to do good. Remember the anti-fugitive slave laws which required persons in the pre-Civil War United States to turn escaped slaves back to their masters. Unjust wars, unjust tax structures, laws permitting pollution of the natural environment, laws permitting abortion on demand—none of these can be changed by good individuals acting out their personal moral lives. One's social conscience, informed by the Word of God, of necessity must act on the system level

—on the political level—and not merely on the individual level.

Finally, even though government cannot change hearts and therefore cannot get directly at the main cause of our social ills, there is much it can do. It can prevent evil hearts, dominated by self-love, from acting out their hate and self-love in acts which defraud and hurt their neighbor, and thereby hurt society. Government, as will be shortly noted, cannot create the perfect society and probably not even a great society, but it can create a better society. And that is nothing to be thrown away.

Earlier we saw that American conservatism to a large degree practices a traditional conservatism. To the extent it does, it approaches complex societal problems with no guiding standards. Here the problem inherent in a split between ideology and practice, in this case between a classical liberal ideology and a traditional conservative practice, asserts itself. The heart of the problem is that classical liberal ideology no longer fits the realities of twentieth-century United States—both in the sense that extremely limited government would be disastrous in terms of personal freedom and in the sense that it is not politically possible to act on the basis of it. Barry Goldwater's stunning defeat in 1964 shows the political infeasibility of classical liberal ideals in contemporary American politics. Thus the American right, while accepting many of the tenets of classical liberalism, is forced by pragmatic considerations to adopt more of a traditional conservatism in practice. But it is a traditional conservatism born of necessity, not conviction. Thus it is the practice of traditional conservatism without traditional conservatism's ideology. As a result it is practice without a program.

American conservatism, instead of having a program of its own, basically plays a holding action, either opposing what the liberals propose or supporting a more limited, scaled-down version of what the liberals are proposing. This pattern has held true in one policy area after another: payment of medical bills, pollution control, aid to education, social security programs, job training programs and so forth.

The difficulty with this standardless approach to policy making is that it leads to opposing programs which should be supported and giving partial, begrudging support to programs which should be opposed. Policy making really passes out of the conservatives' hands, and the initiative rests with the liberals. Conservatism becomes not much more than the liberalism of ten or fifteen years ago and the conservative program becomes not much more than the liberal program cut in half. Thus conservatism, at the outside, can be no stronger than American liberalism; and liberalism has its own peculiar failings and shortcomings.

The door to the prison of American conservatism's own making clangs shut: To the extent American conservatism follows its classical liberal tenets it leads to weak, ineffectual government which leaves the individual vulnerable to the machinations of private economic and social systems; to the extent it compromises its tenets and accommodates itself in traditional conservative fashion to liberal reformism, it embraces a normlessness which does not even attempt to analyze American society and to give guidance to it. To no small degree the political malaise infecting the United States today can be laid at the feet of American conservatism and its inability to give guidance to our age and to offer a viable alternative to American liberalism.

American Liberalism
In one respect American liberalism is easier to analyze than American conservatism, for American liberalism

falls clearly in the tradition of revisionist liberalism and democratic socialism, while American conservatism, as we have seen, is a confused blend of classical liberalism in theory and traditional conservatism in practice. Three basic assumptions underlie American liberalism and tie it directly to the revisionist liberal tradition.

Three Assumptions. The first assumption of liberalism is the belief in the basic goodness of man, or at least in the benign neutrality of man's nature. Usually this belief is not expressed as explicitly as it was by Senator Edmund Muskie when he declared he believed in the infinite moral perfectibility of man.[30] Usually it is held more implicitly than that. Yet it is there. Michael Harrington has written that American society needs

> action to create an environment in which it is more "natural" to help one's fellow man than to profit from him. ... For as the social, non-profit and aesthetic sectors of the society expand, more and more people will be able to live their lives and express themselves in the actual practice of a cooperative, rather than a competitive, ethic. And that fact will be the most powerful sermon of all.[31]

The implicit assumption is that people—given the right environment—will live in natural cooperation and mutual help. Given the opportunity man's goodness will flower.

The second assumption of American liberalism is that freedom cannot be achieved simply by the absence of government regulation. Freedom means the actual opportunity to live a full, creative life, and anything which denies that opportunity denies freedom. Political scientist Robert Dahl, for example, gave expression to that conception of freedom when he wrote that "extreme inequalities in income such as now exist in the United States mean extreme inequalities in capacity to make personal choices effective, and hence extreme inequalities in individual freedom."[32] This assumption in liberal thought sometimes blurs into a more general humanitarianism—a sense of concern and sympathy for all who are economically and socially disadvantaged and a desire to make their lot in life better.

Added to these first two assumptions is a third which, while often implicit in the thought of the earlier revisionist liberals, has received renewed emphasis among today's liberals. It is a strong tendency toward environmental determinism—the belief that man's behavior is determined by his environment. Thus Ramsey Clark has claimed, "Healthy people in a just and concerned society will not commit significant crime."[33] His solution to the crime problem logically follows:

> The basic solution for most crime is economic—homes, health, education, employment, beauty. If the law is to be enforced—and rights fulfilled for the poor—we must end poverty. Until we do, there will be no equal protection of the laws. To permit conditions that breed anti-social conduct to continue is our greatest crime. We pay dearly for it.[34]

The Liberal Program. These three assumptions have led American liberals to espouse and work for strong government intervention in social and economic problems. Whether the program is labeled a New Deal, a Fair Deal, a New Frontier or a Great Society the goal remains the same: to create a humane society marked by equality of opportunity and therefore by a rebirth of freedom. And this is to be achieved through the active intervention of the national government in economic and social affairs. The hope and the expectation are to abolish poverty and want, to end racial and sexual discrimination, and to guarantee the same opportunities to all—whether one is a child of a black ghetto dweller or a wealthy industrialist. The American liberal sees man naked, cold and oppressed, and political action as the quickest and most effective means of supplying clothing, warmth and opportunity.

In the 1960s, aided by the idealism ignited by the Kennedy administration, then by the sense of national unity and sympathy created by Kennedy's assassination, and finally by the rout suffered by the conservatives in 1964, American liberalism gained a preponderance of political power and enacted a significant number of programs. Civil rights acts sought to guarantee blacks first-class citizenship rights, and a whole series of programs declared war on poverty with unconditional surrender as the goal.

But in the 1970s it has become almost fashionable to criticize the liberal enthusiasm and many of the liberal programs of the 1960s.[35] Many are becoming convinced we should recognize that "in politics . . . intentions and consequences are poorly correlated, and idealism has never been a protection against that."[36] And many are coming to agree with Peter Drucker that "there is mounting evidence that government is big rather than strong; that it is fat and flabby rather than powerful; that it costs a great deal but does not achieve much."[37]

Something has gone wrong. Glittering promises seem to have turned to ashes, and high hopes to despair. From out of these ashes voices are asking what has gone wrong—and what is to be done.

American Liberalism: An Evaluation. There are three errors American liberalism has made which, I believe, largely explain why so many of its hopes and programs have gone awry. To understand the present American political malaise it is essential to understand these errors. The first is a tendency to underestimate the complexities and difficulties of the problems it seeks to correct and to overestimate the ease with which they can be corrected. A liberal tends to feel that no problem is so intractable, no challenge so great, but that with enough will and enough intelligence an answer can be found and implemented. John Kennedy's stirring call to put a man on the moon by the end of the decade and the successful meeting of this challenge is a model of how the liberal enjoys thinking and acting. This is the spirit David Halberstam described in the beginning days of the Kennedy administration: ". . . If those years had any central theme, if there was anything that bound the men, their followers and their subordinates together, it was the belief that sheer intelligence and rationality could answer and solve anything."[38] Daniel P. Moynihan has written of the same spirit:

> Wishing so many things so, we all too readily come to think them not only possible, which very likely they are, but also near at hand, which is seldom the case. We constantly underestimate difficulties, overpromise results, and avoid any evidence of incompatibility and conflict, thus repeatedly creating the conditions of failure out of a desperate desire for success.[39]

Given liberalism's assumptions it is not surprising that it makes this first error. To someone sincerely caring about his fellow man and believing that man is basically good or at least morally neutral and that man's behavior is largely determined by his environment, solving problems such as poverty, crime and ignorance becomes relatively simple— somewhat akin to putting a man on the moon. All that is required is to use technology to remove the assumed causes of the problem. Ignorance is solved by establishing enriched educational programs, poverty is eliminated by improving economic opportunities for the poor, crime is solved by improving social conditions. But all fail because ignorance is more than an educational problem, poverty more than an economic problem and crime more than a social problem. Inherited characteristics, deeply ingrained attitudes, psychological impairments, child-rearing patterns, peer-group pressures—all grafted onto a sinful human nature prone to an excessive self-love which is inherently antisocial—create a complexly woven fabric which is hard to unravel. Liberals as a result end up prescribing remedies nowhere nearly commensurate to the problems they are seeking to solve. Black urban ghettoes, for example, are the end product of two hundred years of the most brutal slavery the world has seen[40] followed by one hundred additional years of discrimination and exploitation, all of which is borne by men who share inherently imperfect natures with all other men. To expect that these ghettoes can be liquidated in ten years of limited government programs is simply naive.

A second error in the liberals' approach to policy formation is a tendency to blur or not even recognize the distinction between charity and justice. I am using *charity* in the dictionary meaning of the word: "benevolence and goodwill shown in broad understanding and tolerance of others and generous forgiving or overlooking of their faults and failures."[41] Charity connotes a sense of giving without looking too closely at whether or not there is a basis which justifies giving to the recipient. The motive is love or mercy, and therefore the plight or need of the recipient is enough to provoke charity. I am using *justice*, on the other hand, in the sense I defined earlier in this book: the apportionment of rights and obligations which maximizes true human freedom.[42] Justice thereby connotes providing one with that which is his due because of his humanity. The motive is a sense of righteousness or fair play, based on the worth and value of man.

Often a sense of charity and a sense of justice will lead to the espousal of the same political policies. This is especially true when one recognizes, as I do, that many societal forces threaten personal freedom and thus justice often requires political regulation of these forces and the overturning of their consequences. Yet there is a difference.

Charity is less discriminatory and more promiscuous. It sees a need and hurries to provide a political solution. Justice is more discriminatory, recognizing that there is not a political solution for every wrong and that each political action entails the imposition of obligations or disadvantages as well as the awarding of rights or advantages. It seeks to maximize true freedom, which comes from the proper balancing of rights and obligations. Justice thereby emphasizes the provision of freedom or opportunity; charity, being less discriminatory, often leads to direct subsidy, with the only justification required being the apparent need of the recipient. The tough questions of priorities and of long-range implications for personal freedom and obligations to others are never even asked.

Several problems result when charity is substituted for justice. They all grow out of the basic fact that failing to distinguish clearly between charity and justice strips the policy maker of a clearly defined standard for judging the advisability of government intervention. The choices to be made are tough; the standard used in making the choices is soft and sentimental. One must remember that the number of those in need—those who face difficulties and could benefit from government subsidy—is almost infinite. And they are all clamoring for government help.

Lacking a self-conscious, tough standard with which to evaluate and rank competing programs and policies, the all too real tendency is either to support them all or to bargain with the competing points of view in an attempt to reach a mutually acceptable accommodation. In the first instance one avoids making the hard choices by giving a little bit to everyone. Everyone is kept happy, supposedly, by throwing everyone at least a sop. The Model Cities program, originally intended to be, as the name implies, a small number of pilot projects in a few, select cities, has been expanded to include over a hundred cities. Moynihan has described the non-policy making which went into the formation of the War on Poverty program of the 1960s:

> My impression . . . is that this opposition [of Moynihan] . . . helped produce the December 1963 stalemate in the planning of the program, a stalemate Theodore Sorenson could not or would not resolve, which led President Johnson to call in Sargent Shriver, a completely neutral party, to impose some order on the warring principalities that are sometimes known as the Federal government. . . . Shriver's approach, the logical one, was to adopt some portion, at least, of everyone's program. The result, as I have elsewhere written, was "not a choice among policies so much as a collection of them." The Labor Department's employment program became Title I of the bill. The Budget Bureau's community action program became Title II. And so on.[43]

Closely related to this approach of giving a little to everyone is the approach of bargaining with the various potential recipients of government aid in order to reach a mutually acceptable accommodation. Under this approach those potential recipients with the most political clout tend, of course, to receive the most advantages; those with little clout, the least advantages. Government charity therefore often goes not to open up new opportunities for disadvantaged groups but to preserve the advantages and increase the security of already advantaged groups. Farm price supports, subsidies to the railroads and subsidies to shipping lines all fit into this category.[44]

In the process government encourages inefficiency and incompetence. The railroads and shipbuilders seem to spend more time lobbying for additional favors than they do in developing better management techniques. And this is as it always will be. Charity, while sometimes necessary as a temporary expedient and on rare occasions on a permanent basis for those permanently unable to help themselves, tends to degrade the persons receiving it and to reward inefficiency and incompetence at the expense of efficiency and competence. Thus to the extent government provides charity it encourages the development of attributes in many of its citizens which make men less creative, less valuable contributors to society.

Whether the policy maker seeks peace by giving something to everyone or by bargaining with the interested parties, he is making policy decisions without a clear standard to guide him. The only standard charity recognizes is need, and since needs will always be unlimited—and the resources available to government limited—the decision maker is left with no standard to guide him in establishing priorities and making his choices. The end result is action without goals, purpose or meaning. Theodore Lowi expressed it well:

> Liberal governments cannot plan. Planning requires the authoritative use of authority. Planning requires law, choice, priorities, moralities. Liberalism replaces planning with bargaining. Yet at bottom power is unacceptable without planning.[45]

A liberal means well, but good intentions are no substitute for hard-headed choices among competing alternatives, choices based on rational standards. In the process the status quo tends to persevere by default, and inefficiency and incompetence are protected.

Liberalism's optimistic assessment of man, which the Christian sees as being unfounded, leads it into a third basic error: the assumption that government and the men who run it are benign and trustworthy. As discussed in chapter 3, the dilemma is that the very force the liberals create in order to solve social and economic problems—that is, the government—is infected with the same disease as the social and economic problems: man's excessive self-love. Businessmen, for example, exploit consumers through deceptive advertising and shoddy goods because they are dominated by self-love, so a government regulatory agency to protect consumer interests is created. But to assume that the regulatory agency executives will be any more benevolent and selfless than the business executives is not warranted. And in practice the all-too-frequent pattern is for agency executives to succumb to the influence of powerful vested interests and to lose sight of the broader public interest.[46]

In recent years the tendency found in most of the liberal programs has been, as Theodore Lowi has pointed out, to delegate very broad powers of implementation to the administrative agencies.[47] Both the Water Quality Improvement Act of 1970 and the Clean Air Act of 1970, for example, enunciated noble sentiments and lofty purposes but turned over the creation of most of the actual standards to administrative agencies. The bills, among other things, provided that the President could designate marine discharges other than oil which fell under the terms of the act, authorized demonstration projects for the elimination of water pollution from mines, required the administrator to set standards for aircraft emissions and authorized the administrator to set standards for all potentially dangerous emissions from new automobiles.[48] To turn such enormous discretionary power over to administrative agencies is to reveal a trust in the good will and selflessness of administrators which is staggering. Experience indicates that all too often the trust liberals have placed in the benevolence of administrators has been misplaced. Yet liberals, with their basic faith in man, tend naively to assume that government will serve the ends it is intended to serve and that governmental officials will not be vulnerable to self-centeredness, the influence of the powerful and other human frailties.

In summary, the Christian view of man and society suggests that many liberal programs have failed to reach their objectives because liberals have failed to realize the complexity of many of the problems they have sought to solve, have lost sight of a firm, discriminatory standard to guide their choices and have failed to realize that the men in government responsible for carrying out programs are highly susceptible to reneging on the original intent of programs.

New Left Radicalism

During the 1960s a new movement emerged to challenge the old beliefs of both the left and the right. Growing out of and feeding upon the trauma, violence and turmoil of the 1960s, the new left, a widespread, multi-faceted movement, sought to move beyond the reformism of liberalism into the revolutionary change of radicalism. This movement is difficult to analyze because of its many different facets, its sudden rise, its lack of a clear ideology and now its sudden decline. But it is important to come to at least a basic understanding of it, for even though it has recently declined (especially as a political movement) its impact on American politics continues to reverberate.

The New Left and American Liberalism. In spite of major differences between the new left and old left liberalism, these positions share two basic assumptions. One is a belief in the goodness of man. The new left radical and the establishment liberal both see the source of the evil they observe in society lying outside man's nature. The Port Huron Statement of the Students for a Democratic Society declared, "Nor do we deify man—we merely have faith in his potential."[49]

The new left also shares with liberalism a driving concern for freedom in a broad sense—freedom from economic and social as well as political repression. (As we shall shortly see, however, some new left spokesmen have severely qualified their commitment to political freedom.) This concern for human freedom is a theme which runs through almost all of the new left literature.

The "New" in the New Left. To understand how the new left differs from the old left it is important to note that the new left was molded more by historical circumstances than by ideology. Growing out of the "Beats" of the 1950s and the theories of social change of the Students for a Democratic Society (SDS) of the early 1960s, the new left was tempered by battles fought in the dusty towns of Mississippi, in the universities—first Berkeley, then Columbia and then around the nation—and in the streets. From the early 1960s, with the adoption of the Port Huron Statement by the SDS and the beginning of the southern civil rights struggles, to 1970 and the killings at Kent State University—a period of less than ten years—the new left was repeatedly racked by traumatic events. The murder of civil rights workers in the south and the refusal of the federal government to intervene, the Free Speech Movement at Berkeley, rebellions at Columbia University and other universities, the escalating war in Vietnam, the violence in the streets of Chicago during the 1968 Democratic convention—events always seemed to outrun the development of an ideology. The press of activist struggle did not allow the luxury of theorizing.

In addition, the impact of existentialist authors made experience seem more important than theory anyway. Tom Hayden once declared, "We start armed only with questions, believing that the answers can be discovered in action. You don't invent blueprints and try to conform to them."[50] Action leads to values, not values to action. The Harvard *Crimson,* in an editorial, clearly reflected this emphasis upon experience:

Action is its own reason for existing. Rebellion can only be understood by a rebel who knows that the only "rea-

son" for rebelling is the pleasure (or whatever feeling)
of rebelling itself.[51]

Both the theoretical placing of experience over theory as
the way to truth and the hammering of events themselves
caused the new left to zig and zag as it ran the gauntlet of
events. As the new left developed, however, three strains
of this thought and action stood out.

One was a commitment to what came to be called *participatory democracy* and all that it stood for. The cover of
the 1964 edition of the SDS's Port Huron Statement head-
lines these words:

We seek the establishment of a democracy of individual
participation governed by two central aims: that the individual share in those social decisions determining
the quality and direction of his life; that society be orga-
nized to encourage independence in men and provide
the media for their common participation.[52]

Men were seen as being "infinitely precious and possessed
of unfulfilled capacities for reason, freedom, and love. . . .
Men have unrealized potential for self-cultivation, self-
direction, self-understanding, and creativity."[53] Yet to
those in the new left the achievement of this ennobling
vision of man was being thwarted by the established political powers of the world: Southern blacks were held in
poverty and stripped of their civil rights, mass production
workers and university students were deprived of their
individuality, and third world countries were held in the
grip of an imperialism which guaranteed dehumanizing
poverty. The answer was participatory democracy: means
which would enable all individuals—whether southern
blacks, students in large universities, production line
workers or Vietnamese peasants—to make the basic
choices which affect their lives and in general to wrest
control over their lives from the impersonal forces of a
mass society.

108

This vision of a new world received shock after shock as its young supporters took it out into a world not ready to accept it: Racism and bigotry yielded slowly if at all, university administrators appeared as unyielding as southern racists, appeals to workers fell on deaf ears, the war in Vietnam escalated, and everywhere the police harassed and hounded.

These frustrations and failures encouraged two further strains in the new left movement: a violent, antidemocratic tendency and a tendency toward withdrawal from political activism. The inability to arouse mass support among workers and the poor (the new left was largely composed of white, middle-class intellectuals) led to the espousal of antidemocratic sentiments. The people have been deluded by those in power and therefore must be led. They must be purged of the reactionary ideas the system has taught them. To accomplish this there should be tolerance for some ideas, intolerance for others.

Liberating tolerance, then, would mean intolerance against movements from the Right, and toleration of movements from the Left. . . . True pacification requires the withdrawal of tolerance before the deed, at the stage of communication in word, print, and picture. Such extreme suspension of the right of free speech and free assembly is indeed justified only if the whole of society is in extreme danger. I maintain that our society is in such an emergency situation, and that it has become the normal state of affairs.[54]

Meanwhile the failure of the political system to respond favorably to the political demands of the new left led to the espousal of violence and a tendency on the part of some even to glorify and romanticize violence. Violent revolutionaries such as Ho Chi Minh and Che Guevara were exalted. Theoretician Howard Zinn defended the limited use of violence.[55] And Herbert Marcuse wrote:

But I believe that there is a "natural right" of resistance for oppressed and overpowered minorities to use extra-legal means if the legal ones have proved to be inade-quate. . . . If they use violence, they do not start a new chain of violence but try to break an established one.[56] The late 1960s also saw a growing tendency for the new left to withdraw from political activism into a subculture of its own, marked by drugs, relaxed sexual mores, acid rock, new hair and dress styles, experiments with communal living arrangements, and, for some, religion. Charles Reich's 1970 best-selling book, *The Greening of America*, saw the new left as essentially a cultural, not a political, movement: "There is a revolution coming. It will not be like revolutions of the past. It will originate with the indi-vidual and with culture, and it will change the political structure only as its final act."[57] Despairing of changing the political system, many new left radicals took the option of dropping out and creating their own subculture.

Today the new left as a movement is clearly in decline. Its political activism has dissipated, and its cultural inno-vations have been gutted by society's co-opting its surface manifestations while ignoring its deeper critiques of mate-rialism and racism. Yet the new left's radical critique of American politics and society continues to be debated, and it continues as a significant force in American society.

New Left Radicalism: An Evaluation. The new left has made a real contribution to American political discourse by broadening the concept of personal freedom. It espe-cially has done so by showing how both racism and the impersonal forces of a technological age have limited man's creative opportunities. It is hard to deny that the racism, materialism and dehumanization of American society are real. American society continues to move "toward two societies, one black, one white—separate and unequal."[58] The large universities were—and often are—

110

in need of a greater appreciation of individual student needs and contributions. The mass assembly line factories worship at the shrine of high productivity and profits rather than at the shrine of worker welfare. It sometimes seems as though society is dedicated to the proposition that materialism is the highest value and that neither other persons nor the natural environment ought to stand in the way of one's pursuit of prosperity. The credit card should perhaps replace the flag as the national symbol. To the extent the new left's critique of American society has sharpened our awareness of the personal poverty that can accompany material prosperity, the stultifying effects of racism and dehumanization, and the threat of environmental pollution, we have all benefited.

In spite of these contributions, the new left represents no more of a guide to political and social renewal in the United States than do conservatism and liberalism.[59] It merely leads us from one swamp to another. Its insistence on locating the basic source of evil in corrupted social, economic and political systems instead of within individual man himself is its most basic error. This results in an overemphasis on participatory democracy as a sort of modern-day patent medicine which will cure all political, social and economic ills. The heart of the new left's faith is that if existing institutions and patterns can be destroyed and direct participation of the people substituted, the people will work out new patterns which will be free of racism, greed and exploitation. Thus it is unnecessary for the new left to spell out a specific program: The new will arise naturally from among the people once they are given their freedom. And the new will be good, since man's goodness will be free to act and mold society.

But it requires a monumental faith in the innate goodness of man to believe that if stripped of existing restrictions he would choose good over evil, a sense of equity over racism, mutual respect over exploitation. The Christian view of man insists, and experience confirms, that to assume free, individual men will necessarily choose the right and good and equitable is naive. Chapter 2 demonstrates that there is something innately wrong in man which makes him so aggressive, so concerned with self, that a society based on respect and understanding is impossible. But this is the very basis on which the new left expects to build its new order—through the mechanism of participatory democracy. To seek to do so is to build without a foundation.

There is a lesson to be learned from the fact that following the 1968 presidential elections and the criticisms of the nominating process engendered by it (especially from the new left) several states adopted new or greatly strengthened presidential primary elections. The first of these new primaries held in 1972 was in Florida. It was won by George Wallace, the political figure most opposed to what the new left represents. Therefore the new left, before destroying the old order—racist, corrupt and exploitive though it may be—should be able to show with what it would replace it and why there is a basis to expect it to be an improvement. Participatory democracy as an end in itself is not enough.

The new left's failure to create a counter culture true to its own goals and ideals is itself testimony to the intractableness of the moral imperfections in man. The Woodstock music festival in August of 1969 was largely a success, but by the summer of 1971 the music festivals which followed it were marked more by thefts, delays, violence and confusion than by love, togetherness and peace. By 1972 they were no longer even being held or were merely commercialized copies of the originals. And the communes established by new left disciples ended in failure more often than success. The dilemma inherent in these communities is summarized in the words of a letter to the *Modern Utopians:*

> If the intentional community hopes to survive, it must be authoritarian, and if it is authoritarian, it offers no more freedom than conventional society. I am not pleased with this conclusion but it now seems to me that the only way to be free is to be alone.[60]

A second basic difficulty with the new left is a tendency to see the world in overly simplistic, black-white terms, instead of in various shades of grey. New left writings ring with moral indignation against the old order and heady confidence in their own vision for the future. Approaching the world with the simplistic dichotomy of disdain for the old leaders who are all bad and of moral confidence in themselves who are completely right, violence and the limitations of civil rights are all too easy to accept.[61]

Bombing, and the death and injury which sometimes accompany it, burning lifetime research notes of disliked professors and ransacking university offices can only be justified by one who is certain of his own righteousness and his opponents' wickedness. Closely allied to the violence into which the new left has sometimes fallen is the intolerance to opposing ideas, which Marcuse and others have advocated. Those who know what is right and what is moral must lead and teach the people, suppressing false views and tolerating the right views—with themselves, of course, possessing the right views and their opponents the wrong views. A moral arrogance such as this is as dangerous and as stifling as the racism and hate the new left seeks to eliminate.

Christianity, with its teaching of man's limits and sinfulness, warns against assuming the perfect moral righteousness of one's own views. To allow the free play of ideas instead of seeking to enforce one's own ideas through violence and suppression of opposing ideas is essential for a free, orderly society and the justice which flows from a proper order. To argue that the current system is already repressive and violent as a justification for more repression and violence is to take a partial truth and then extend and absolutize it in order to have a justification for one's own repression and violence. True, the old order has elements of repression and violence in it, along with elements of freedom, order and peace. But the new left, absolutizing the former, ignoring the latter and arrogantly assuming the perfect goodness and practicality of their own vision, supported a program of violence and repression which would have plunged society into repression and violence far surpassing that against which they originally revolted.

By a long route we come to the conclusion that the three broad alternatives the current era is offering American society as paths into the future—conservatism, liberalism and new left radicalism—are all dead ends. Ignoring the actual nature and needs of man and seeking to build a post-Christian view of man on the basis of humanism, scientism and existentialism, they turn idealism into despair, hope into fear. A better way is needed.

5
Progressive Realism: A New Option in Domestic Politics

IN THE PRECEDING CHAPTER classical liberalism was criticized because of its overly narrow view of freedom, traditional conservatism because of its lack of standards by which to judge either new proposals or the status quo, and revisionist liberalism because of its overly optimistic assessment of human nature. Furthermore, American conservatism was criticized for its limited view of human freedom, American liberalism for its naive assumption of the benevolence of government, and the new left for its faith in participatory democracy as a cure-all. A plague on all your houses appears to be the emerging message.

But what beliefs or political programs does a Christian have to offer in the place of those he criticizes? Does he have an alternative to the antigovernment outlook of classical liberalism, the overly limited view of freedom of American conservatism, and revisionist liberalism's overestimation of the ease with which economic and social problems can be solved? Does a Christian view of man and politics offer a way out of the box which forces one to choose between the inaction and continuing injustices of American conservatism, the swollen bureaucracy and governmentally frozen injustices of American liberalism, and the disorder and chaos of the new left?

To offer a tight, neatly packaged Christian answer to the issue of the proper role of government in a society's affairs is overly ambitious. For me to do so would violate my own emphasis on the complexity of political issues and the frailties of man (including, of course, myself). Yet I believe certain basic elements of a response in keeping with Christian views of man and society are clear and some of their implications discernible. Therefore, what I offer here is not a complete, well-rounded answer, but movement toward an answer—movement which carries us beyond the alternatives currently being offered and gives hope that the political process can be made to serve justice and freedom more fully than they do now.

What results I call *progressive realism*. It is *realism* in the sense that it attempts to take a hard-nosed, realistic approach to man and society. In distinction from many of the post-Christian views of man, it is not diverted by wishful thinking or selective observations into adopting a romanticized, overly optimistic vision of man. Nor does it reduce man to purely material or animal existence, something to be used and manipulated. It seeks a realistic picture of man: with all his potentialities and limitations, strengths and weaknesses, high purposes and often low achievements. Realism follows wherever biblical teachings and man's best knowledge and most accurate insights lead—whether the conclusions reached are flattering or unflattering to man and American society, and whether they lead to optimism or pessimism about the future of American society and its political system.

116

Yet the approach I develop is a *progressive* realism. It is progressive in the sense that it believes progress is possible and strives to attain it. It is realism with hope and ideals. The Christian ideals of man and society and the God-like purposes for which they were made form the basis for dreams. The marriage of progressivism and realism, of ideals and tough-mindedness is what the modern age needs. For too long we have been led down paths of dreams and ideals without the tough realism which progress demands, or down paths of realism and toughness without the dreams and ideals which rescue us from apathy and the quiet acceptance of injustices. We seek a better way. We seek a progressive realism.

THE BASIC ELEMENTS

Basic to progressive realism are three fundamental beliefs about the nature of politics and man. The first is an organic concept of society, somewhat similar to what the traditional conservatives stressed. There is increasing evidence that each generation is in fact intimately bound up with both past and future generations and that the old maxim "The past is prologue" is highly accurate. A society's past can be either a prison or a launching pad, but it is becoming increasingly difficult to deny that a society's present, with its attitudes, mores and orientations, is intricately bound up with its past (and therefore of necessity with its future).

Political science's recent surge of interest in nonwestern nations has led it to emphasize *political culture*—a society's basic attitudes, values, assumptions and orientations which are politically relevant.[1] A society's political culture exerts a continuing impact on its political processes, encouraging certain patterns, discouraging others and making some altogether impossible. Robert Ward, for example, in an article seeking an explanation for the abil-

117

ity of Japan alone among Asian nations to modernize economically and politically concluded,

> When evaluating the modernization of Japan, it is useful to keep in mind this long, complex history of covert preparation from which the society benefited. This still stands as a unique accomplishment in Asia, but its roots are buried at least two hundred years deep in the country's social and political history.[2]

And David Apter explained different patterns of modernization in Ghana and Uganda on the basis of the distinctive types of traditional culture which had evolved in the two countries.[3] Many of the political differences among the United States, Britain, West Germany, Italy and Mexico have been explained on the basis of their distinctive political cultures, which in turn can be explained by the differences in their social and political histories.[4] This latter study supports the conclusion that probably the most important factor assuring the success or failure of free, democratic government is not legal forms and procedures but the society's culture and the deeply ingrained values, attitudes and expectations which make it up.

For our present purposes the significance of the crucial role political culture plays in a nation's politics lies in the fact that culture is organic by its very nature. It can be neither created nor destroyed by law or edict. It evolves. One generation, through the socialization process, passes on its culture to the next. Change—while not absent—is resisted.

> Although culture is more complex than a simple summing operation . . . culture is essentially a product of individual values systems. Since individuals resist change in their values, the societal culture is also seen as resistant. . . . Culture resists change in its composition.[5]

Thus culture normally evolves over a long period of historical development and change; it is not created anew each generation. It is also worth noting that in this socialization process, this passing on of values from one generation to the next, the family plays a particularly significant role.[6]

In summary, what any government can and cannot do is significantly influenced by the political beliefs, values and orientations of its society—beliefs, values and orientations which are the end product of a long evolutionary process and are preserved by their transmission from one generation to another, a transmission in which the family usually plays a major role. We may think this organic nature of society and politics to be good or bad, we may accept it or reject it, but it is still true. To ignore it is as foolhardy as for an engineer to ignore the law of gravity.

This organic conception of society is at variance with both the classical and the revisionist liberal's concept of a society amenable to the will of man, a society man can change and manipulate by his will and action. The organic conception of society says society is too complex, is made up of too many strands and is too resistant to change for that sort of bald manipulation. Thus society and its culture both create certain potentials on which the political system can capitalize and certain limits on what the political system can do. The political system must take societal values and traditions into account. To do otherwise is to court disaster and to assure ineffectiveness.

The second basic belief about man and politics fundamental to a Christian political response is the peculiar combination of goodness and evil inherent in man's nature. As noted in chapter 2,[7] man is inherently inclined toward an excessive self-love yet is capable of goodness and a selfless love. Thus a Christian approach to politics is not a politics of despair: Man is not absolutely corrupt. Yet neither is it a naively optimistic approach. Something is tragically wrong with man, something which seems to frustrate all of man's best intentions and noble deeds.

Thus a Christian approach to politics must be tough, taking into account the evil and problems into which man's excessive self-love often leads him. Yet it is also careful not to slip into a hopelessness which despairs of individual or societal improvement. Although all men, and thereby all societies and governments, are affected by sin, all men, all societies and all governments are not equally affected by sin. This is basic to understanding the motivation for Christian political involvement. Some persons' minds and wills have become so twisted by self-love that they have surrendered to a hatred which hurts all those with whom they come into contact, while others have reached a relatively high level of self-giving love so that they are marked by a concern and respect for others which helps all those with whom they interact.[8] So also societies range from that of the Ik, an East African tribe marked by cruelty and a loveless disdain even for each other,[9] to those of modern-day Norway or New Zealand, which are characterized by relative virtue and mutual respect. And governments vary from those which are cruel, repressive and destructive of individual liberties, such as totalitarian Nazi Germany and Stalinist Russia, to relatively enlightened, freedom-defending governments, such as modern-day Switzerland and Luxembourg.

This means that even though realism demands a large degree of pessimism about man and his potential for good, it also accepts the possibility of progress (as well as, of course, of regression). There are real gains to be made and real losses to be prevented. As stressed earlier, politics cannot create the perfect society and probably not even a great society, but it can create a better society. And that is nothing to be thrown away. To argue otherwise is to argue that there is no difference between Nazi Germany and democratic Switzerland.

Thus progressive realism differs from both the classical

and the revisionist liberals, with their belief in man's essential goodness or at least moral neutrality. Such a belief flies in the face of human experience as well as Christian teaching. Progressive realism comes close to traditional conservatism on this point, although it is more careful to recognize both the potential for good and the power of evil active in human affairs, and thereby the potential both for progress and for regression.

A third element basic to progressive realism is the proper role of politics outlined in chapter 3. The evangelical Christian—starting out with the belief that man is created in the image of God himself—sees politics possessing the mandate to seek a just order, that is, to assure each man his due, by maximizing true freedom. True freedom is viewed in a broad, realistic sense, as the actual opportunity to develop and use one's creative capacities in keeping with God's law of love. The just order in which this true freedom is maximized is seen as emerging from the proper balancing of rights and obligations, free choices and limitations on free choice.[10]

This means that progressive realism sees government playing a broader, more active role in society than did classical liberalism, with its concept of freedom as being infringed only by government action. In distinction from traditional conservatism, Christianity gives progressive realism a standard or norm which leads to goals and ideals against which to evaluate present and proposed programs. And in distinction from American liberalism the norm is justice and freedom, and not a less precise, more sentimental charity, which is unable to discriminate among competing demands for political action.

It is out of these three fundamental elements that progressive realism's more specific response to societal needs and problems emerges. These three basic elements inform the more specific elements of a Christian political response.

MORE SPECIFIC ELEMENTS
An Active, Interventionist, Humane Politics

The first element in the politics of progressive realism is a commitment to an active, interventionist, humane politics. The oppressions, the sufferings, the exploitations present in society are recognized for what they are. The powerful grind the poor and powerless into the dirt, majority groups create a closed system into which minority group members have no access, and the rich use their wealth to live in a surfeit of self-centered luxury. To refuse to see these oppressions and this decadent self-centeredness or to see them and fail to be moved with concern and a righteous anger is to deny the inherent worth of all persons and the sense of justice which flows from this inherent worth.

The Bible commands a different attitude. Old Testament prophets such as Isaiah and Amos condemned the rich for their idleness and oppression, and sympathized with the poor and downtrodden; Jesus Christ mingled with the poor, the prostitutes and the outcasts of society, and he warned the rich that their chances of entering his kingdom were less than the chances of a camel to pass through the eye of a needle. Typical of the Bible's attitude toward the rich is James' angry denunciation of the rich who exploit their workers:

> Come now, you rich, weep and howl for the miseries that are coming upon you. Your riches have rotted and your garments are moth-eaten. Your gold and silver have rusted, and their rust will be evidence against you and will eat your flesh like fire. You have laid up treasure for the last days. Behold, the wages of the laborers who mowed your fields, which you kept back by fraud, cry out; and the cries of the harvesters have reached the ears of the Lord of hosts.[11]

In the light of this witness everyone should bleed for every hungry child, for every family head denied the right to support his family by gainful employment, for every family torn apart by a senseless war. To live a safe, contented life, protected by a shell of private affluence and social myopia, is to support injustice; to reach out in love, to bind up wounds, to root out the cause of the wounds, is to support justice.

But this is not necessarily a plea for political action. To identify the need to reach out to the oppressed and powerless with the need to engage in political action is to slip into an error which liberals have often made. There are social ills for which there are no political solutions. But by the same token there are some social ills for which there are political solutions—or at least political means by which to make real improvements. The sympathetic and active concern for others is what should be present. Whether that concern ought to lead to political action or to some other type of action remains an open question.

To determine whether or not one's sense of moral outrage at a social or economic ill should lead to the adoption of a particular proposed political solution, it is necessary to answer three questions. First, is the social or economic ill resulting in a loss of freedom for a segment of society? This question asks (given the concept of freedom developed in this book) whether or not, as a result of the alleged ill, persons are being deprived of the opportunity to make choices freely, to mold and shape their lives as they desire to do. Normally the answer to this first question will be yes, for almost every economic or social ill reduces the range of free choices a person can make.

The second question is more difficult: Would the proposed political solution to the freedom-reducing ill result in a net gain of freedom for society? This question is crucial for its answer determines whether or not the proposed solution will strike the balance between rights and obligations, between guaranteeing free choice and limiting free choice, which leads to an increase in true freedom in society. Two things need to be weighed here: the relative number of persons who would gain rights or advantages and obligations or disadvantages, and the relative importance and value of the rights or obligations, advantages or disadvantages, being imposed. (Value and importance are here judged, as noted in chapter 3, in light of God's law of love.) As the number of persons who would gain rights or advantages goes up and the number of persons who would gain obligations or disadvantages goes down, and as the importance and value of the rights or advantages being gained goes up and the importance and value of the obligations or disadvantages being imposed goes down, the likelihood that society would experience a net gain in true freedom increases.

The third question asks whether or not some other alternative (either political or nonpolitical) is available which would result in a larger net gain of true freedom for society.

Thus for government to adopt a new program in an effort to meet a social or economic ill three conditions should be met: (1) the social or economic ill must result in a deprivation of freedom (a condition almost always met); (2) the proposed political solution must lead to a net gain in true freedom for society; and (3) the proposed political solution must lead to a larger net gain in true freedom for society than other political or nonpolitical solutions. It is by weighing these three factors that one determines whether or not a proposed program will strike the balance between rights and obligations which will lead to the maximization of true freedom, which, in turn, is the defining characteristic of a just order.

I must confess I recoil from such a formal, almost mathematical formulation of a standard, as though elements such as freedom, rights, obligations, social ills and political solutions can be neatly packaged and weighed. Clearly they cannot. Thus developing a standard such as this and applying it in concrete situations are not the same. Even those agreeing on a standard will often reach different conclusions when applying it because of biases, disagreements over the facts in a specific case and different perspectives. Yet starting out with the standard given above, one is ahead of the person who starts out with an improper standard or with only his unarticulated, perhaps even unconscious, feelings and predispositions. He has at least clarified his goals and standards. Where he ends up—while not fully determined by any means—is nonetheless significantly affected.

By making true freedom the element basic to the standard, the standard grasps the element most needed for a humane, just society. Freedom in the sense of actual opportunities to act as a willing, creative, loving being is what assures that man can be fully man, that he can attain the heights of love and creativity for which God created him. Thus a politics with true freedom as its goal is a just, humane politics. And freedom, by its very nature, can only be maximized by a balancing of rights and obligations, advantages and disadvantages, free choice and limitations on free choice. It is not an entity that can be freely distributed in society with no costs incurred. The adoption of the standard proposed here does not guarantee a just, humane politics, but it does, I believe, improve the chances that a more just, more humane politics will be achieved.

Perhaps the use and nature of the standard given here can be clarified by two brief case studies: The first illustrates how the standard can lead to what is usually considered a liberal policy, and the second illustrates how the standard can lead to what is usually considered a conservative policy.

Case Study I Health Care. All persons are susceptible to

illness and accident. Suddenly the previously healthy person finds himself physically incapacitated by disease or mishap. Prior to modern medicine, illnesses and accidents were simply endured since no one could do anything much about them anyway. But with the advent of modern medicine, and increasingly as medicine improved its capabilities, man was able to fight back against disease. Diseases are being conquered and life prolonged.

But there is a price tag to this progress. Many of the new lifesaving procedures are enormously expensive, requiring hospitalization and the use of expensive drugs and equipment. Health care costs in the United States rose from 12 billion dollars in 1950 to 75 billion dollars in 1971 —more than a sixfold increase![12] Even as a percentage of the gross national product, which grew rapidly from 1950 to 1971, health care costs rose from 4.6 per cent to 7.4 per cent. Although the government's Medicare and Medicaid programs cover the major medical expenses of most of the elderly and many of the poor, and although many persons are partially covered by private insurance plans, serious illness or accidents still mean economic disaster for many. This fact was recently illustrated by a story carried by the New York Times' news service about a couple whose daughter had leukemia. Added to the tragedy of the illness itself were financial worries. Despite the father's working night and day, the parents were described as not knowing what to do and fearful of the future. The mother was quoted as saying,

It costs $150 to $175 a day in the hospital and $200 a day in isolation. I've seen bills for $4,000 and $7,000 and $9,000 going through. I don't know what we are going to do now, how we are going to be able to pay the bills in the future. We just can't pay half those amounts. I've seen what happens to other people when their insurance runs out. I'm worried.[13]

126

One point is clear: Illnesses which reduce a family to poverty levels, saddling them with a debt which will take years to pay, are destructive of important, valuable personal freedoms. Both parents in a family may be forced to work or the main breadwinner may be forced to put in long overtime hours. Small joys—opportunities to travel or to do volunteer work, time to spend with the family, participation in community activities—must all be foregone as one struggles to survive financially. And over the entire family hangs a debilitating sense of worry. The opportunity for living a creative, loving life is seriously curtailed. All this comes about, not because of unwise or foolish choices the persons have made—no one chooses to be sick—but because of unknown and uncontrolled factors of heredity and circumstance.

Clearly a government program which would pay health care costs would reduce or eliminate completely the crush of financial disaster by spreading health care costs evenly throughout the population. In that sense those afflicted by major medical expenses would gain advantages which would make them more free than they are now. But that does not settle the issue, for the advantages gained must be weighed against the obligations or disadvantages—and therefore the loss in personal freedom—that would be part of the costs of the program. All would lose some personal freedom (or gain disadvantages) in the form of higher taxes; all would have less income to dispose of at will. Insurance companies, hospitals, doctors and others closely involved in the present health care structure would also lose in that they would have to conform to the new program. The extent to which their present practices, which may be very appealing to them for financial or other reasons, would have to be changed would depend on the exact nature of the government program and would no doubt vary with the role the person fills in the health care structure. Insurance companies would probably be affected the most, but many people would incur obligations they do not now have.

Thus the question resolves itself into one which seeks true freedom by weighing the freedom the population generally gains by eliminating large, crippling medical bills against the disadvantages imposed on all of us through higher taxes and on those in the insurance and health care fields who would have to conform to the new regulations. Given the relatively small number of persons who would gain substantial disadvantages (largely those in private health insurance companies), given the relatively small disadvantages most persons would gain (largely health care personnel and all of us as taxpayers) and given the important, valuable advantages many families with major illnesses would gain, I judge that such a government program would result in a net gain in true freedom for society. More persons would gain more important, valuable advantages than would lose advantages. A comprehensive, government-sponsored health care program would, in other words, mean that Americans would be free to live more creative lives, with more opportunities to exercise discretion in directing their affairs.

Case Study II: Crime and Punishment. Consideration of a second issue further illustrates the workings of the standard for political intervention and in this case illustrates how its application does not necessarily lead to what is generally considered a liberal position. What type of ideals and goals should motivate our handling of convicted criminals is the issue I wish to explore.

Concerning the first criterion of the standard, it is clear that our present means of handling convicted criminals reduces personal freedom. Persons in prison or other correctional institutions most obviously are losing personal freedom. And indirectly society is losing freedom also—

through the loss of tax money used to support the prisons and through the high rate of recidivism. Some forty per cent of released prisoners are returned to prison for additional crimes within three years of their release.[14] To the extent previously convicted criminals, whether sidewalk muggers or bank embezzlers, continue to pursue their criminal activities we all lose some measure of personal freedom. We become afraid to walk the streets at night or we conclude we can no longer trust the claims of a business, and thereby our freedom to walk the streets or to utilize the services of a business is curtailed.

Presently two alternative approaches are being offered to the question of punishment for criminal activity. One basically views criminal activity as a sickness to be treated and cured. It stresses reformation and rehabilitation of the criminal and makes use of various social-psychological therapies, combined with the indeterminate sentence. The latter is a sentence which does not consist of a set time interval but which lasts until the criminal is judged cured. If his attitudes toward society and his behavior improve quickly, he will be released quickly; if his attitudes and behavior do not improve, he remains in prison. He has not yet been cured and needs additional help.

The second basic approach to punishment stresses that the criminal should be required to pay for his crime. This view sometimes has been described as retribution, in the sense that society works vengeance on the criminal. But this is really a caricature of this position since it connotes a hardness and heartlessness which is not inherent in the concept. Rather, the emphasis should be on the idea that each of our acts carries certain consequences with it. Thus a criminal act carries certain consequences. The criminal hurts not only his specific victim or victims, but all of society. He has attacked the bonds of civility which make society possible. Thus justice says he owes a debt to society which he must pay. Punishment then becomes exactly that—not an enforced curing of an alleged sickness. To be fair this punishment must fit the crime. It must not be hard or vindictive, but its severity must be reasonably related to the seriousness of the crime committed.

Liberals have tended to support the rehabilitation concept with the indeterminate sentence and to oppose the punishment concept. They see the former as being humane and understanding, and the latter as harsh and perhaps even barbaric. We should understand and help, not punish. This approach fits nicely with the liberals' emphasis on the importance of environmental factors in molding man. After all, it is a criminal's environment which led him to crime—which caused his sickness—and thus the understanding thing to do is not to blame and punish him, but to rehabilitate him, to cure him of his environmentally caused illness.

But the difficulty with the rehabilitation concept is that it is, in fact, more inhumane, more dehumanizing, imposes greater obligations on a prisoner and therefore is more destructive of personal freedom for a prisoner than the punishment concept. As a recent study prepared for the American Friends Service Committee declared, "Suffering within the penal system has not decreased. The opposite seems to be the case: rehabilitation has introduced a new form of brutality, more subtle and elusive."[15] Some indication of the actual nature of the indeterminate sentence is revealed by the fact that the average prison stay is longer under the indeterminate sentence than under sentences of a set number of years.[16] Worse, the criminal loses much more personal freedom under the indeterminate sentence than he loses when he is punished by being required to pay a set fine or spend a set number of years in prison. He is told, under rehabilitation, that he has a disease which he himself may deny is a disease, and then his personality and his will are assaulted with the tools of modern psychotherapy. He is treated as something less than a man, for he is manipulated in ways we normally reserve for animals.

This manipulation becomes especially sinister when, as is often the case today, the victim is poor and black, and the "therapist" or "correctional officer" is middle-class and white.

> The paternalism implicit in A's assumption that he knows better than B what is for B's benefit is treacherous under any circumstances and becomes an intolerable form of colonialism when invoked by middle-class whites to run the lives of blacks, Chicanos, Indians, and the poor.[17]

Jessica Mitford has cited the case of

> an Indian prisoner in San Quentin serving an indeterminate sentence of one to fifteen years for burglary; as a first offender, he would ordinarily have been paroled after a year or so. For eight consecutive years the parole board refused to set a release date because he would not go to group therapy.[18]

On the other hand, the punishment approach, when of a reasonable, humane nature, imposes less severe obligations on the prisoner, and thus results in a smaller loss of freedom, than the rehabilitation approach. To be punished is to be told that you made a choice and here is the consequence; and the consequence is the same for you as it would be for anyone else performing the same act and it is commensurate with the offense you committed against society. It should be one's acts which determine his punishment, not some white, middle-class expert who judges if he is now good enough to live again in society. Thus he is still a man. He is not simply an object to be manipulated. He is paying for a choice he made; he is not being manipulated like an animal. He is still free to choose his future paths.

C. S. Lewis summarized the case clearly,

It may be better to live under robber barons than under omnipotent moral busybodies. . . . Their very kindness stings with intolerable insult. To be "cured" against one's will and cured of states which we may not regard as disease is to be put on a level with those who have not yet reached the age of reason or those who never will; to be classed with infants, imbeciles, and domestic animals. But to be punished, however severely, because we have deserved it, because we "ought to have known better," is to be treated as a human person made in God's image.[19]

Now this does not mean that prisons ought to be inhumane institutions where the convicts are dehumanized, subjected to threats and harm from fellow prisoners, and given no opportunities. They do not need to be "country clubs," but they should be fairly run, with decent, humane conditions prevalent. Various services, such as opportunities for education and for learning new skills, should be available for those who desire them. And for those with adjustment and psychological problems counseling services should be available. But to force someone to use these services, to undergo rehabilitation and to make his release dependent on some expert declaring him rehabilitated is to strike at the heart of being human. The conclusion is that punishment imposes less severe obligations or disadvantages on a prisoner, and therefore results in a less severe loss of freedom for him than does the rehabilitation approach.

One additional facet of this issue remains. Perhaps a prisoner's greater loss of freedom which characterizes rehabilitation and the indeterminate sentence would be justified if it resulted in greater freedom for society at large. If rehabilitation did a much better job of preventing additional criminal acts by persons released from prison than does the punishment approach, then one might conclude that society overall is gaining in true freedom. For then the loss in personal freedom—the disadvantages and obligations—suffered by convicted criminals would be more than offset by the greater personal freedom the rest of society would gain through the reduction in criminal activities. But all indications are that rehabilitation does not reduce recidivism more than the punishment approach does.[20]

Thus the substituting of rehabilitation for punishment, therapy for justice, in fact leads to a paternalistic, patronizing hold on the criminal that is dehumanizing and harsh—and is of no real value to society at large.

In summary, progressive realism promotes an activist, interventionist, humane politics, but not a promiscuous interventionism or activism. It is a measured interventionism, with the standard of true personal freedom being the guide. Hopefully, a paternalistic, big-brother politics is thereby avoided; hopefully a cold, uncaring politics is too. A government should care and care deeply, but its goal is freedom of choice and opportunity, not an enforced sameness where all—whether through government force or through government largess—are expected to be marked by a similarity of achievement, attitude and style of life.

A Cautious Politics

A second element of progressive realism is a cautious, watchful attitude toward public policy making which prefers to feel its way rather than suddenly to jump into a wholly new policy. Many political scientists have stressed the fact that policy making is typically a never-ending process of policy formation, reaction, modification, further reaction, further modification and so on.[21] Incremental policy making is the result. Change is attained by a series of small steps as an existing policy is adjusted or modi-fied, reactions set in, further adjustments are made and so on. This policy making by increments, rather than by sharp breaks with the past, is the normal pattern of policy mak-ing because of the very nature of the American political process. But there are also good theoretical reasons in sup-port of this procedure. As Charles Lindblom has pointed out, making only incremental or marginal changes in policy often increases the effectiveness of the policies made, because such an approach

1. concentrates the policy-maker's analysis on familiar, better-known experience;

2. sharply reduces the number of different alternatives to be explored; and

3. sharply reduces the number and complexity of factors he has to analyze.[22]

Particularly when viewed in the perspective of the organic nature of society, the infinite complexity of social prob-lems, and man's moral imperfections and finite abilities, incremental decision making has much to commend it. If social problems were simply caused by one or two factors which were easy to isolate, radical breaks in current pro-grams would be easier to justify. But when, in fact, the causes of a social problem are likely to be an intertwined net of dimly perceived factors, some of which are deeply embedded in the culture of a society; when significant facts are unknown or in dispute and the consequences of proposed alternatives uncertain; and when man's judg-ments are likely to be distorted by his self-interest and pre-conceived notions, incrementalism has much to recom-mend it.

Incrementalism compensates for the complexity of social problems and man's finiteness by, as Lindblom ar-gued, sharply reducing the number of factors to be weighed and considered. Incrementalism also assures that one can learn from previous steps before he takes the next one, as he considers past strengths and weaknesses, successes and failures. And the moral or judgmental errors that are made will be smaller, with less severe consequences, than if broad, new policies were being implemented.

One alternative—or supplement—to incrementalism is the use of pilot programs or test programs, in which several alternative policies are tried out in real life but limited situations, the results studied, and then the most promising alternatives adopted as national policy. Here again the principle is to feel one's way, take one step at a time, weigh the results and then adjust one's actions before the next step is taken.

The big danger in elevating incrementalism to a principle is that incrementalism is constantly threatening to degenerate into simple preservation of the status quo or at the most into changes that are so small as to be almost meaningless. Then incrementalism becomes a means to block meaningful change, not a means to promote it. And the opponents of change often seek to use incrementalism in this manner.

But the type of incrementalism I believe should be part of a Christian approach to politics is a rolling incrementalism which constantly and self-consciously presses ahead. The next step is being planned before the first step is completed. The image ought to be that of constant, rolling movement rather than that of quiescence until forced to move and then the smallest movement possible followed by a reinstatement of quiescence.

This rolling incrementalism typifies the spirit which underlies the Christian approach to politics I have termed *progressive realism*. It struggles and works for progress; it is not satisfied with things as they are. In its Christianity it finds a force which compels a concern for the problems

135

and failures of society. Yet its Christianity also warns against simplistic solutions and cure-all patent medicines. It therefore moves slowly and deliberately—but it does move. It thereby rejects both conservatism's accommodation to the status quo and liberalism's and new left radicalism's belief in instant utopias.

Built-in Administrative Checks

The third specific element in progressive realism seeks to recognize the all-too-great ease with which political institutions and processes can be turned away from the good intentions for which they were created. As pointed out earlier, the inclination toward evil within the hearts of men causes the need for political regulation and control, but it also affects the men who write and administer political programs, often leading them to turn the original intent of a program down paths of self-interest.

Thus progressive realism suggests that a variety of checks ought to be built into public policies and the apparatus created to administer them in an attempt to assure that they will in fact not be turned aside from the purposes for which they were enacted. Men who are disadvantaged by a public policy will be seeking to influence those who administer the policy, and because of frailties and excessive self-love all men share, administrators of policies all too frequently make easy marks. The fact that political administrators normally operate away from the light of publicity and often deal with one interest instead of a multiplicity of countervailing interests makes them particularly vulnerable.

As a consequence, there is a tendency for administrative agencies to go through a fairly predictable life cycle: The agency initially exercises its powers in a strict, vigorous manner, but then gradually succumbs to the influence of certain special interests and loses sight of the broader public good. One professional economist, for example, after studying the Civil Aeronautics Board and its regulation of the airlines, concluded, "Here an agency of Government has proved itself a willing instrument of vested carriers seeking to maintain a closed industry."[23] The evidence indicates that administrators of policies in the executive branch of government are more prone to short sightedness, more likely to become pleaders for narrow interests and more subject to conflicts of interest than are White House officials, congressmen and judges.

The type of administrative checks I have in mind could take many different forms. Perhaps the most effective and basic one would be for Congress to delegate less discretionary power to the administrators of policies, specifying more exactly the standards and terms of a policy. As noted earlier[24] the recent tendency of Congress, in the face of increasingly complex and technical issues, has been to state the basic goal of a piece of legislation, set a few limits and then give the bureaucracy an almost free hand in setting the exact standards to be implemented. Administrators of policies are of necessity a part of the policy making process, but the broad delegation of policy decisions to the bureaucracy has given unprecedented policy making powers to the very persons who have proven most susceptible to social myopia, conflicts of interests and the outright trading of favors to which all men are prone.

Another type of check which could be built into the administrative process would be to place a time limit on a public program and its bureaucratic apparatus—say a ten- or fifteen-year time limit—after which the program automatically self-destructs, unless renewed by the legislature. This would place the burden of building support and demonstrating the need for the program on its proponents and would at the least lead periodically to a thorough, public review. Without such a time limit simple inertia favors retaining whatever programs are in existence now, whether they are good, bad or indifferent.

A final type of check would be to create within the bureaucracy an elite, top-level corps composed of persons with high ability and a sense of identification with and loyalty to the corps (rather than to the administrative department in which they may be serving). In order to foster loyalty to the corps rather than to any particular agency, these officers should be shifted from one department or agency to another every four or five years. In order to assure their loyalties would not be to outside, private interests, from whom they may have come a few years ago and to whom they hope to return in a few years hence,[25] they should be highly paid, and other devices should be used to encourage their permanent employment in the corps. These persons would be less susceptible to either institutional myopia, which places a higher value on defending and aggrandizing themselves and their agencies than effectively serving the broader public interests, or to conflicts of interest between their regulatory role as a public official and their sympathy and perhaps identification with the interests they are charged with regulating.

Thus a Christian view of man and society leads to a politics I have called *progressive realism*. It is *progressive* in that it believes that progress is possible through political processes and that the effort to move ahead should be made, and it provides a standard by which to judge political intervention in society. Yet it is *realism* in that the Christian perspective—with its organic view of society and relative pessimism about man's nature—limits intervention, insists on modest, step-by-step progress, and calls for checks and safeguards on those who administer programs. Although progressive realism is not a complete political program, it does avoid many pitfalls current alternatives have fallen into and sets us on the right path.

Politics in the
World Political Arena

III

6
From Fulbright to Kissinger: International Political Options

A GENERATION WHOSE SENSIBILITIES have been numbed by the body counts and kill ratios of Vietnam, and whose minds are unable even to comprehend the full horror of threatened nuclear war, hardly needs to be persuaded that American foreign policy is failing to cope effectively and prudently with the mounting problems in the world political arena. Just as the scientism, humanism and positivism of today have led American society's domestic policies up a dead-end alley, so also they have led American foreign policies up equally barren paths. Watergate, inflation, urban decay and pollution at home are matched by Vietnam, dollar crises, a nuclear balance of terror, and a growing gap between the rich and poor nations abroad. Nowhere was this more evident than in Vietnam. We used all the best tools our modern learning and technology had given us: computers, systems analysis, highly sophisticated weapons and psychological profiles. But we could not even ask the questions which begged to be asked and answered—questions of morality, proportion and purpose.

Thus we return to a basic theme of this book: that the political alternatives being offered Americans today are morally and politically bankrupt. I have argued this theme in the previous chapter in relation to domestic policies; it is no less true in relation to international politics. Again I am convinced that the values and insights of historic, evangelical Christianity offer the basis for a new way, a way which would be an improvement over the wasteful, barren foreign policies currently being pursued by the United States.

This chapter first considers very briefly the basic issues present in the world political arena (those issues which are challenging American foreign policy) and then considers the nature of international politics and how it differs from domestic, or intranational, politics. Next the basic approaches to the creation of foreign policy currently vying for domination are considered. In the following chapter the basic ingredients of a better way, a way informed by Christian values and insights, are explored.

THE WORLD POLITICAL ARENA: THE ISSUES

Three basic issues are confronting American foreign policy. The success or failure of American foreign policy depends on its successes or failures in dealing with them. Our current feeling of malaise in foreign policy largely stems from our inability to come up with sound responses to these three basic issues.

The first of these issues is the perennial question of war and peace. How best to preserve the nation's security from foreign military attack and how best to promote peace is the issue. Throughout man's history there seems to be no goal which man has more earnestly desired and more frequently failed to achieve than peace. Peace is the universal longing, war the constant reality. No other aspect of international politics has been the subject of more research, analysis, speculation and writing.

With the arrival of nuclear weapons of mass destruction and both land- and sea-based missiles, the issue of war and peace has escalated from a question of the safety and prosperity of societies to the question of the very survival of the human race. Science has given us the Bomb, but it has not given us the means to control it.

The second issue concerns how the United States ought to react to the injustices and tragedies found throughout the world. These range from the stifling of the freedom of intellectuals and artists in the Soviet Union to brutal, authoritarian military regimes in Brazil and Chile, from massive starvation in northern West Africa to the inhumanity of apartheid in South Africa, from wretched poverty in much of Latin America to the 1968 foreign invasion of Czechoslovakia. The list is endless. It seems as though wherever one looks in this world one can find political or racial repression, economic injustice or natural disasters. The issue raised by them is what, if any, responsibilities does the United States have to right these wrongs and to use its influence to make the world more humane, more just. Some of the confusion which exists relative to this issue is seen in the fact that many of the same persons who attacked American military involvement in Vietnam on the grounds that we should recognize the limits of our power and not try to right all the wrongs of the world, now call for the United States to take the lead in applying economic sanctions to South Africa in order to force its abandonment of apartheid.

The third problem challenging the United States is how to react to difficulties posed by an increasingly interdependent world.[1] Pollution and other abuses of the environment are threatening the entire planet with disaster. Environmental abuses know no national boundaries and therefore cannot be solved by purely national actions. And to a degree still not realized by many persons the United States has become dependent upon the importation of certain raw materials to sustain its standard of living, which in turn makes it necessary for the United States to find markets for its exports in order to maintain a reasonable balance between imports and exports. In addition, huge multinational corporations—both American corporations with investments in other nations and foreign corporations with investments in the United States—have added to the interdependence of the world.

The threat of pollution, dependence on foreign sources and markets, and giant multinational corporations all point to a world in which American well-being is intimately tied in with events and decisions taking place throughout the world. For the United States to dominate these events and decisions would require it to dominate the world, which is practically impossible and morally unacceptable. But to remain passive and merely to accept as given events and decisions affecting basic American interests is also unacceptable.

These are the key challenges facing American foreign policy in the next ten to twenty years. The alternative sets of assumptions and outlooks which are currently being offered as bases for American foreign policy are, I believe, inadequate to meet these challenges effectively and prudentially. Something better is needed. But before specifying more exactly the shortcomings of the current alternatives and the outlines of a better way, it is necessary to understand more about the nature of international politics.

INTERNATIONAL AND INTRANATIONAL POLITICS

To understand American foreign policy—both its failures

and potentials—it is necessary to have some understanding of the realm of international politics in which American foreign policy must act and react. There are both similarities and differences between the world of international politics and the world of domestic, or intranational, politics, but the differences clearly outweigh the similarities. In many ways we are operating in a new ball game when we shift from intranational to international politics, and we need to be clear on the ways in which the rules of the game have changed.

Authority

Clearly the most significant difference between *interna*tional and *intra*national politics is the absence of authority in international politics. As I emphasized in chapter 3, the existence of authority is the key distinguishing mark of government and politics. Government was defined as the social institution which possesses the right to make authoritative decisions for an entire society and politics as the process of making authoritative decisions for an entire society.[2] The existence of authority is the crucial element.

But in the international arena there are no institutions or persons who are accorded legitimacy, who possess authority over the some 180 nation-states. To be blunt, anarchy exists in the international arena. Austin Ranney has accurately described the situation:

> Yet the state system, both in legal principle and in political practice, comes very close to constituting a genuinely anarchical world political system. The principle of sovereignty ... provides that no international law which a nation has not accepted is legally binding upon it. ... There is no world legislature to make laws binding upon all nations, no world executive and police force to make sure that world laws are obeyed, and no

145

world judiciary to adjudicate violations of such law and to sentence the violators. The United Nations General Assembly, is, to be sure, a sort of pseudolegislature, the United Nations Security Council, a sort of pseudoexecutive, and the International Court of Justice a sort of pseudosupreme court. But ... none of these institutions has any real power beyond what the individual nations have given them—and can withhold or withdraw whenever they desire.[3]

Thus the term *international politics*—given the definition of politics used in this book—is really a misnomer. There is no world government, no world political system, and thus no real politics on the international level. There are, of course, numerous contacts and relations among nation-states, and these are what usually are referred to by the term *international politics*. Ambassadors are exchanged, treaties negotiated and international organizations created and kept functioning. Thus the absence of an authoritative government does not mean that total chaos or total isolation prevails among the nations of the world.

In fact, a number of fairly regularized customs or conventions have developed among national governments, some of which have been formally recognized in treaties, which nations normally accept and respect. These customs and conventions constitute what is called *international law*. The according of certain privileges and immunities to ambassadors and other diplomats, certain rules regulating behavior on the high seas and certain international agencies such as the Universal Postal Union (which regulates the international exchange of mail) are all examples. These conventions (or international law), while helping to make an orderly world possible, differ from domestic law in that they rest on voluntary acceptance by the various independent countries. As many are accepted as are because most of them are in the self-interest of all the nations. Often individual nations ignore or disobey them when it is in their national self-interest to do so. Thus nations such as Peru and Iceland, with valuable fishing resources off their coasts, have rejected the previously accepted three- or twelve-mile limit to a nation's territorial waters and have declared their territorial waters to extend far out into the ocean (two hundred miles in the case of Peru and fifty miles in the case of Iceland).

Conflict

In chapter 3 we saw that different individuals pursue conflicting goals on the intranational level and that politics is one means of resolving these conflicts.[4] Without conflict there is no politics. International politics also involves conflicts; but here the parties are nation-states, not individuals, and politics is not an available means of resolving these conflicts. Thus other means of resolving conflicts—negotiation and coercion—are used at the international level.

Through regular diplomatic channels, summit meetings of heads of state, special negotiations on specific issues, and the United Nations' or other international organizations' channels, national governments frequently get together and seek to resolve conflicts through the negotiating, bargaining process. Especially when nations possess a reservoir of good will, a tradition of working together and a common cultural heritage, such negotiations are often successful.

Sometimes coercion is resorted to in an effort to resolve international disputes. War is, of course, an example. But often threatened or actual coercion of a nonviolent nature is also used. A nation may be persuaded to curtail exports to another country by that country threatening to impose import quotas if it does not do so, as the United States has done with Japan. Or a trade embargo can be placed on a certain country in an attempt to force a change in policy, as many have urged be done to South Africa to persuade it to change its apartheid policy. Nonviolent coercive pressures are brought to bear in an attempt to compel one nation to do the will of another.

Often negotiation and coercion are used in conjunction with each other. Negotiations are pursued while coercive actions and threats are used as a means of forcing concessions in the bargaining room.

What is called *international politics*, is, therefore, not the process of making authoritative, enforceable decisions by some supra-national institution, but the process of negotiations and coercion by which nations seek to resolve their conflicts.

An additional factor, however, makes international conflicts often more difficult to resolve than domestic conflicts. Persons living in two different countries tend to be divided not only by nationality but also by language, cultural and racial or ethnic tradition, religion and economic level.

Thus finding common ground and establishing a sense of mutual respect is particularly difficult in relations among national governments. Man's sinful nature—his excessive self-love—fractures all human relationships, but the danger of that fracture turning into an unbridgeable gap is particularly great when it involves relationships across cultural, historical, linguistic and economic divisions. It is difficult enough for a man to love someone as himself, but it is particularly difficult to love someone of a different culture, color, religion and economic level.

Thus the resolving of conflicts on the international level is made difficult both by the absence of authoritative institutions and processes, and by sharp, often bitter, conflicts among nations and their peoples. Tensions, threats and war all too naturally result. Yet a Christian, constrained by the love of Christ, feels the necessity to make the effort to do better. The rest of this chapter explores and evaluates the basic approaches being advocated as ways of constructing a safer, more orderly world out of the anarchy-prone, tension-filled world political arena.

TWO DIMENSIONS IN FOREIGN POLICY MAKING

Underlying the reactions of foreign policy-makers—and their critics—are certain basic assumptions about man, morality and the nature of international politics. To the extent American foreign policies have failed—and failures are not hard to document—the cause ought to be sought first of all in the basic assumptions and perspectives which have informed the more specific American foreign policies. Thus this section of the chapter sorts out two basic dimensions underlying the specific foreign policy stands of the United States: liberalism-conservatism and idealism-realism. The following section then combines these two dimensions to form the four basic approaches which are currently vying for domination. The failures and the loss of direction in American foreign policy noted earlier can largely be explained by the failures and short-comings of these basic approaches.

Liberalism-Conservatism

The liberal-conservative dichotomy, which plays a crucial role in domestic policy debates, is also present in foreign policy debates, but in a somewhat altered form. For the most part liberalism and conservatism—growing out of the traditional conservatism, classical liberalism and revisionist liberalism of Europe—have been oriented toward issues of domestic politics and not toward issues of world politics. They have been concerned with issues of individual freedoms, governmental power and rate of change, not with military deterrence, national security and international order. Nevertheless, liberalism and conservatism play a role in the development of American foreign policies, and their differing assumptions and outlooks have led to distinguishable approaches to foreign policy making.

Liberalism. Three basic marks of American liberalism distinguish it as an approach to foreign policy. First is liberalism's assumption of the basic goodness of human nature. As was true of both the classical and revisionist liberals, American liberals see mankind in a benign, optimistic perspective. Man is basically good; social, economic and political institutions in his environment are what make him bad.

The second mark of American liberalism relevant to foreign policy making is its belief in the possibility, even the likelihood, of progress. Liberalism is an optimistic creed. Almost unlimited progress is attainable with enough effort and good will.

The third basic mark of American liberalism relevant to its foreign policy stance is a strong commitment to freedom and justice. The liberal weeps for the starving children of Biafra, the imprisoned and tortured priests of Brazil, the wretched poor of Buenos Aires, the repressed blacks of South Africa. The liberal, with his strong commitment to human dignity, reacts to injustice and repression wherever he encounters it. His compassion does not stop with the United States' borders.

The basic nature of American liberalism which, on the domestic level, leads to support for strong, active government, leads on the international level to support for an active, interventionist foreign policy. Believing in man's goodness, eternally optimistic about human progress, and repelled by injustice and repression, a liberal sees his government and its foreign policy as a readily available tool to right wrongs present in the world. An example of this liberal spirit is provided by Senator Edward M. Kennedy in his article on the Northern Ireland situation:

> There are those who say that America should stand silent in the face of the daily tragedy taking place in Northern Ireland. I do not agree, and I do not think that most Americans agree. Our heritage as citizens in a nation that has been a spokesman for peace and human liberty in the world for two centuries requires us to speak out and find a helpful role to play in contributing to a permanent peace in Ulster.[5]

Evangelical Christianity certainly supports the liberal in his concern over injustice and repression. As I will emphasize more fully later, Christianity deemphasizes the importance of nations and national identity. What is important is the human individual made in God's image. This is what gives him worth and makes him a proper recipient of justice. Whether he is an American or Mexican, Nigerian or Swede, is really not that important. Thus a liberal's pushing his concern over human well-being beyond the borders of his own country is right and proper.

But where liberals go wrong is in their overly optimistic assessment of human nature and therefore their overassessment of the ease with which injustice and repressions can be overcome. Just as on the domestic level a liberal underestimates the difficulty of overcoming longstanding problems, problems rooted in man's own intractable, imperfect nature, so also on the international level he underestimates the difficulty of overcoming problems and evils, which are also rooted in man's sinful nature. And on the international level he faces the additional obstacle of there being no authoritative institution—no government—which can seek to correct wrongs and to bring justice. The net result is a tendency toward promiscuous interventionism and a dissipation of efforts. Too little for too short a time becomes the all-too-real tendency, whether the program is foreign aid to a corruption-riddled government or a few Peace Corps volunteers scattered around a country of millions. With results overpromised, hope soon gives way to despair. Liberal efforts end up being marked by starts and stops, first one program and then another, as promised results fail to materialize.

Liberalism also runs the danger of degenerating into a moral arrogance in which it is assumed that Americans know what is best for the world—whether the problem is civil war in Nigeria, terrorism in Northern Ireland, apartheid in South Africa or birth-control policies in Latin America. The ever-present temptation is to intervene into little understood, morally ambiguous, and essentially internal, affairs of other nations. Although a liberal's moral sensitivity to human suffering and injustice is most commendable, the danger that this sensitivity will degenerate into a moral arrogance and a promiscuous interventionism is great.

Conservatism. At the opposite end of the continuum from liberalism is American conservatism, with its peculiar mixing of classical liberalism and traditional conservatism.[6] The overriding characteristic of American conservatism as it relates to foreign policy is its nationalism. The classical liberal concept of the free, autonomous individual struggling for his own welfare and survival with neither help nor hindrance from the government is on the international level translated into a fiercely independent, strong United States making its own way in the world. The individual free from governmental restraints on the domestic level is matched on the international level by a United States strong enough to act without the restraint of other nations.

This underlying commitment to an independent, strong United States has led to three more specific outlooks: a strong sense of pride in the United States and belief in its virtue and accomplishments, a belief in the need for strong military forces and a belief in the need for the United States to pursue its own national self-interest. The sense of pride in the nation is an international manifestation of classical liberalism's individualism and sense of pride in oneself and one's accomplishments won by hard work and effort. Strong military forces are what help assure a strong, independent nation—and fit in with the self-assured, "I can take care of myself" spirit of American conservatism. The defense of national self-interest is an international counterpart to the classical liberal belief that each individual should pursue his own economic self-interest.

Thus American conservatism as it relates to foreign policy is dominated by its classical liberal roots, not by the elements of traditional conservatism which appear in its domestic policy. Traditional conservatism's beliefs in the imperfections of man, the organic nature of societies and the need for gradual change are overwhelmed by classical liberalism's belief in individualism and the need for the pursuit of individual self-interest.

Thus American conservatives normally support higher military budgets, believe in the use and threatened use of military force, are suspicious of accommodations with other nations (especially the communist governments of the Soviet Union and China), and oppose strong involvement in the United Nations or other international organizations which might compromise national sovereignty.

Conservatism's strong nationalistic tendencies run counter to Christianity's emphasis upon the value and worth of all men regardless of nationality. In the story of the Good Samaritan Jesus taught (among other things) that acts of love and mercy ought not to be limited by the bounds of nationality. And in general the Bible hardly takes an exalted view of nations and their pretentions. The

153

prophet Isaiah may have put it in more extreme words than the Bible usually uses, but his words reflect a more general biblical emphasis: "All the nations are as nothing before him, they are accounted by him as less than nothing and emptiness."[7] George Kennan summarizes Christian teaching well when he writes:

> This institution of the sovereign national state,... whatever its secular justification, has no foundation in Christian principle. Nowhere in Christ's teachings was it suggested that mankind ought to be divided into political families of this nature, each a law unto itself, each recognizing no higher authority than its own national ego, each assuming its interest to be more worthy of service than any other with which it might come in conflict. Surely this whole theory is an absurdity from the Christian standpoint.[8]

Certainly Christianity also teaches the importance of nations and their governments. The prior chapters have argued consistently that they are a vital means of enforcing justice and order in human society. But one ought not to make one's own nation into an idol—as a conservative tends to do—to be placed ahead of all other values. The nation is to be valued, but the sense of loyalty, significance and support given it is to be balanced by a sense of concern for other nations and their rights and problems. The conservative does not err in respecting his nation, in respecting strong military forces or in defending his country's interests. As I will develop more fully later, these emphases are needed in an imperfect, fractured world. But they must be balanced by a love and concern for all humanity and the need to seek justice for all countries and peoples. This the conservative tends not to do.

Idealism-Realism
Partly overlapping and yet distinct from the liberal-con-

servative dimension is a second dimension of basic attitudes and outlooks in foreign policy formation: the idealist-realist dimension. Liberalism and idealism, and conservatism and realism overlap in several respects. Yet the differences are sufficient to make it helpful to conceive of the idealist-realist dimension as a separate dimension.[9]

Idealism. Idealism—sometimes also called *utopianism* or *moralism*—starts out, as does liberalism, with a strong belief in the basic goodness of human nature. We are once again back to the never-say-die faith that says, in spite of all the evil and inhumanities man wreaks upon himself, man is basically good.[10]

This belief makes possible the key distinguishing mark of the idealist outlook: the belief in the power of rationality and ideals. One idealist put it this way:

> True nations and true men live by their spiritual values and ideals. They will go to jail, starve or die before they will betray these ideals ... [and] the only foreign policy, therefore, which will work is one that wins men and nations by the ideals and spiritual values for which it stands.[11]

Reason and moral force, in other words, are seen as a powerful tide, having the potential to sweep away injustices, repressions and archaic practices. To the idealist, large armies and a jealous guarding of national self-interest are not necessary. What is needed is education, communication, good will and a rational thinking through of problems. If we treat the other person reasonably and fairly, he will respond in kind. As Ernest Lefever expressed it, idealism emphasizes

> the rationality and moral capacity of man and the possibility of continuous or cumulative progress in history. This approach, which has instructed a great number of religious leaders, has emphasized the ideal goals of international peace, justice, and brotherhood. Advocates

155

of this approach often insisted upon an absolute ethic based exclusively upon goodwill, noncoercion, cooperation, and education.[12]

Idealists often slip into a rigid moralism, an acceptance of one or more basic moral principles which they then apply rigidly in any and all situations and conditions.[13] And with an almost touching naivete they believe that their vision of morality and goodness will prevail merely because it is (in their view) moral and good. Thus the idealist who has slipped into moralism may, for example, condemn the use of force in international politics anywhere, anyplace, or he may take the principle of self-determination and apply it rigidly to any and all circumstances irrespective of possible ameliorating conditions. The idealist is prone to slip into moralism since, operating in the world of ideals and goals, he takes what may be an ideal goal and, forgetting the torturous path to be traversed to gain it, immediately and simplistically applies it to any and all circumstances.

Christians have frequently had idealist tendencies. Especially the social gospel school of liberal American Protestantism, with its optimistic view of man and belief in progress, has tended to support idealism. But evangelical Christianity is clearly opposed to idealism. In an imperfect world, with men and nations acting selfishly and often irrationally, to expect noble sentiments and lofty ideals to carry the day because of their inherent logic and virtue is naive. Lefever was correct when he wrote,

American liberal idealism, including its Christian and Jewish manifestations, seems to be more closely related to eighteenth- and nineteenth-century secular thought than to the views of the ancient Hebrew prophets, the early Christian church, the Medieval church, or the teachings of the Reformers.[14]

Evangelical Christianity has always taught that the world

is a tough, difficult place, where moral ambiguities abound, man's evil nature remains unbridled and virtue is not its own defense. In some respects idealism is the international equivalent of anarchy on the domestic level. Both believe that in the absence of force, order based on morality and goodness will emerge. Earlier I argued that on the domestic level the authority and force of government are needed; later I will argue that on the international level, in the absence of authority and government, means of self-defense and coercive power are needed.

Realism. Challenging idealism as an approach to foreign policy formation is realism, an approach that has for the most part been in ascendancy among American foreign policy makers since World War II. Realism starts off with an avowedly pessimistic view of human nature. George Kennan, a leading proponent of realism, has written of "man's irrational nature, his selfishness, his obstinacy, his tendency to violence."[15] And two scholars have described realism's view of man in this way:

> In contrast to utopianism, realism holds that human nature is essentially constant, or at least not easily altered. Man is not innately good or perfectible. There are severe limitations in the extent to which political reform or education can alter human nature. Man is evil, sinful, power-seeking.[16]

The realists' pessimistic assessment of man leads them to argue that coercive power is what affects the course of world politics, not noble ideals. Rivalry, struggle and strife are the ingredients of international politics. The strong walk over the weak, for there is no international system of law or government to uphold the rights of the weak.

Thus the realist concludes that each country must defend its own national self-interest by means of national coercive power. National interest thereby becomes the goal

157

of foreign policy, national power the means.[17] Moral principles and self-sacrifice are lost in the pursuit of power and self-interest. Winston Churchill defined foreign policy formation in these terms when he said,

Foreign policy is not a game, nor is it an academic question, and . . . not an ideological question. . . . Foreign policy is in fact a method of protecting our own interests and saving our own people from the threat of another war, and it is against that criterion that the foreign policy of any government has to be measured.[18]

Arthur Schlesinger clearly threw out moral principles in foreign policy making when he wrote, " . . . the safest basis for decision in foreign policy lies not in attempts to determine what is right or wrong but in attempts to determine the national interest."[19]

The realists' position does not argue, however, that the world is necessarily in a state of constant war. It sees negotiations and bargaining constantly going on among countries as they seek to adjust their differences. War is usually not in a country's self-interest—at least if its potential enemies maintain their military strength. Thus the realists see a world of national governments each jealously guarding its interests and building its power, and seeking to resolve its conflicts with other national governments through negotiation and compromise. Morgenthau summarized this view of world politics well:

The concept of the national interest presupposes neither a naturally harmonious, peaceful world nor the inevitability of war as a consequence of the pursuit by all nations of their national interest. Quite to the contrary, it assumes continuous conflict and threat of war, to be minimized through the continuous adjustment of conflicting interest by diplomatic action.[20]

In reacting to the realist position I reluctantly conclude that as a description of what international politics is it in fact is an all-too-accurate description. The starting point of the realists—the tragically flawed nature of man—is close to the Christian description of man's present condition. As I emphasized in chapter 2, man is in fact tragically flawed: He is marked by an excessive self-love which leads to the selfishness, shortsightedness and violence the realists have noted. Thus in pursuing foreign policy it becomes easy for a government to concentrate on merely its own immediate self-interest and to ignore the needs and interests of other peoples. This is what normally occurs in international politics. The rich nations pursue trade policies which help themselves and hurt the poor countries;[21] treaties are proposed not to aid worldwide human progress but to advance one's own nation's welfare;[22] and foreign aid programs are used to build national security.

The difficulty with the realist position is not, therefore, that it misunderstands reality, but that it tends to make what is into what ought to be. To see the avarice and selfishness of the nations as a fact is one thing; to praise it as desirable is something entirely different.

The realists see their position preventing a promiscuous interventionism by the United States based on a moral arrogance that says the American concept of justice ought to be forced onto all humanity—by force of arms if necessary. John Bennett has praised realism for this very reason:

> I have learned especially from George Kennan and Hans Morgenthau the role of national interest as a limiting concept. Both men have continually criticized moralism in foreign policy from the standpoint of national interest. . . . A nation that uses its power to press its moral ideals on other nations is likely to throw its weight around far too much for its good and theirs.

It is easy for Americans to see this in the case of the Communist nations. Do we not breathe a sigh of relief at any sign that Russia is concerned about its real national interests and is less interested in crusading for Communism?[23]

On this basis it is argued that greater morality will be achieved if we pursue our national interest than if we pursue morality. Good comes forth out of evil.

But does it? To argue that there is an area of life where moral principles do not apply runs contrary to the Christian teaching that we should love our neighbor as ourselves. To accept American self-interest as the sole guiding principle of American foreign policy is to ignore the exploitive practices of American corporations in Latin America, to support authoritarian rule in Greece, to ignore mass starvation in northern West Africa. Christ's story of the Good Samaritan teaches that my neighbor is anyone who needs my help and whom I am in a position to help, regardless of barriers of nationality and tradition. A man is a man; he is created in God's image and thereby respect is due him. And the biblical principle that "every one to whom much is given, of him will much be required"[24] would seem to apply to the United States, with its potential for vast influence in the world. Later we will see how this morally motivated concern ought not to be used to justify an unlimited interventionism. Moral principles must work themselves out within a proper framework, but that does not alter the fact of their relevancy to foreign policy decisions.

Many of the realists who criticize the application of moral principles in foreign policy are in fact attacking a straw man of their own making. Arthur Schlesinger, for example, has argued against the application of moral principles in foreign policy.[25] At another point in his lecture he supports his case against morality in foreign policy by arguing, "It must finally be observed that few problems in international politics are ever cast in the mold for unequivocal ethical approval or disapproval.... Most issues of foreign affairs do not lend themselves to categorical moral verdicts."[26] But what these last sentences indicate is that what Schlesinger is really attacking is not the application of moral principles to foreign policy, but the application of moral principles in a simplistic, absolutistic manner. He is attacking moralism, not, as he claims, the application of moral principles to foreign policy problems.

It is, of course, true that "unequivocal ethical approval or disapproval" or "categorical moral verdicts" neither can nor should be made in the formation of foreign policy —nor in any other field for that matter. Even in our own personal lives, as well as in foreign policy making, most ethical choices are morally ambiguous.[27] Ethical values clash, our information is sketchy and time is short. This is true of an individual trying to decide whether his responsibility to his family should cause him to stay in his present, stable job, or whether his responsibility to his community should cause him to quit his job and get involved in a financially shaky enterprise active in civic improvement. It is equally true of a foreign policy maker trying to decide whether his commitment to racial equality should lead him to oppose trade with Rhodesia or his commitment to national security should lead him to support trade with Rhodesia in strategic materials.

Life is filled with moral tensions and problems, and this is as true on the personal level as it is on the international level. Neither the individual nor national governments should seize upon one moral principle and apply it indiscriminately and simplistically. Thus Schlesinger and other realists' arguments against the application of moral principles in foreign policy are really not arguments against the reasoned, balanced use of moral principles, yet they ban moral principles in broad, sweeping terms. This evangelical Christianity—with its commitment to God's will ruling in all of life—refuses to do.

There is also a more subtle problem with realism. What at first appears simple is, in fact, so complex that the straightforwardness of realism is lost. The problem is how to define and discover the national interest. Is one to take only what is in the self-interest of the country in a here-and-now, immediate sense? Or is self-interest to be taken in a long-range sense (which might sometimes involve going against the country's immediate self-interest)? In addition, national security from foreign attack and subjugation is about the only goal which is in the interest of all of a society. Normally one course of action will be in the interests of part of society (say, the consumers) and the opposite course of action in the interest of another part of the society (say, the industrialists). Whose interest then is the *national* interest? It probably depends on whether it is your ox or mine which is being gored. In practice the national interest is an elusive, slippery concept, ready-made for manipulation by anyone seeking justification for his favorite policy.

Thomas Cook and Malcolm Moos express the problem well: "Unfortunately, however, present definitions of national interest . . . are in their realism less than realistic."[28] The danger, they go on to argue, is that when national interest is divorced from moral considerations it becomes difficult "to avoid a purely government-inspired formulation [of the national interest], executive and administrative—a concept put forth as the United States' national interest, and in due course turned into a statist line in the name of unity, effectiveness, prestige, and power."[29]

Realism, although avoiding the errors of idealism, clearly suffers from its own shortcomings.

FOUR FOREIGN POLICY PERSPECTIVES
Earlier in this chapter we noted the sense of discontinuity and uncertainty triggered by the Vietnam War and rein-

forced by the rapidly changing world scene. We no longer are so sure of ourselves. We intuitively feel our past foreign policies are no longer adequate—if they ever were—but we are uncertain where to turn.

The need is to cut through this fog of uncertainty and to come to a clearer understanding of where American foreign policy has been, where it has gone wrong and what now needs to be done. In accomplishing these tasks the two previously discussed dimensions of foreign policy, with their differing assumptions, are helpful—but not enough. The secret to understanding currently clashing prescriptions for American foreign policies is to realize that conservatism or liberalism and idealism or realism have seldom worked alone in molding specific foreign policies. Instead, the two dimensions interact together, each affecting and modifying the other. Thus the sets of assumptions and outlooks which have molded foreign policies can best be viewed as combinations of the two dimensions, as illustrated by Figure 2.

Four basic approaches to foreign policy making emerge: quadrant A, the liberal-idealists; quadrant B, the conservative-idealists; quadrant C, the liberal-realists; and quadrant D, the conservative-realists. I have spotted several individuals and movements on the figure to illustrate how they can be ranked relative to the extent to which liberalism or conservatism, idealism or realism informs their foreign policy outlooks. In the following discussion each of the four quadrants is considered separately.

The Liberal-Idealists

Andrew Carnegie once instructed the trustees of the Carnegie Endowment for International Peace,

> When . . . war is discarded as disgraceful to civilized man, the Trustees will please then consider what is the next most degrading evil or evils whose banishment . . .

163

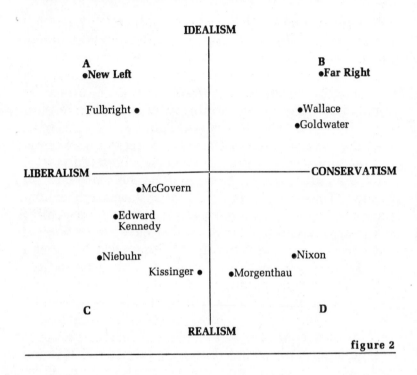

figure 2

would most advance the progress, elevation and happiness of man. . . .[30]

This spirit of boundless optimism and faith in progress typifies, even if in somewhat exaggerated form, the moving spirit of the liberal-idealists.

Beliefs. The liberal-idealists blend liberal and idealist tendencies. They are liberal in their belief in the goodness of man, their belief in progress, their commitment to justice and their opposition to repression throughout the world. They are idealists in their deemphasis on the military and other forms of coercive power and in their emphasis on the power of ideals and rationality. They sometimes slip into moralism, but many are highly sophisticated, perceptive observers and scholars.

From these basic assumptions three basic beliefs emerge. First is an almost boundless faith in what can be achieved. Wars can be stopped, poverty eliminated and freedom assured. This optimistic spirit is reflected in the dedication Lester Brown wrote for his very able book, *World Without Borders*: "This book is dedicated to a world order in which conflict and competition among nations will be replaced with cooperation and a sense of community." Later in the book Brown suggests that the wiping out of poverty throughout the world and the establishment of world government are attainable goals.[31] The liberal-idealists' optimism is also reflected in the Students for a Democratic Society's Port Huron Statement:

> The United States' principal goal should be creating a world where hunger, poverty, disease, ignorance, violence, and exploitation are replaced as central features by abundance, reason, love and international cooperation.[32]

The second basic belief of the liberal-idealists is that the key to progress is the rational application of ideals to the world's problems, with communication and education playing a large role. In the process old values will have to change. Brown writes, "A dialogue of global dimensions must be initiated, encouraged and stimulated as to our mutual plight if a survival ethic and consequent new life style are to emerge."[33] Senator J. William Fulbright sees education playing a crucial role if peace is to be attained:

> What we can and must do is ... to try to expand the boundaries of human wisdom, sympathy and perception. Education is a slow-moving but powerful force. It may not be fast enough or strong enough to save us from catastrophe, but it is the strongest force available for

165

that purpose, and its proper place, therefore, is not at the periphery but at the center of international relations.[34] Peace, in other words, comes not through military might and a balance of power, as the realists claim, but through people's ideals and commitments.

The third basic belief of the liberal-idealists (and this is becoming increasingly true of today's liberal-idealists) is that social upheaval, disruption and sometimes even violent revolution are necessary for the new order of worldwide peace and prosperity to be ushered in. One scholar has written that "planetary humanists," who are close to what I am calling liberal-idealists,

are much more concerned with social change—rather than peace—in a world which they see as beset by dynamically mounting socio-economic crises, and their remedies focus on socio-political reforms. Many of them decry stability and accept the desirability in some cases even of violent change.[35]

The earlier liberal-idealists, especially between the two World Wars, were mainly concerned with peace, international order and the use of supranational organizations to bring peace and order. But today's liberal-idealists— under the impact of liberalism's concern for justice and the growing interdependence of the world—are placing a greater emphasis on worldwide change and social progress.

The outlooks and commitments of the liberal-idealists in practice lead to a fairly wide range of specific foreign policy proposals. There is an especially sharp break between liberal-idealists with new left tendencies and more moderate liberal-idealists. The new left tends toward a demonological view of the world, with American capitalistic imperialism the chief demon.[36] Barnet, for example, argues,

The thesis of this book is that war is a social institution,

that America's permanent war can be explained primarily by looking at American society, and that America's wars will cease only if that society is changed.[37]
Tucker explains further the new left view:

What does explain America's persistent expansion, in the radical view, is a socio-economic structure. America's interests in the world are the necessary outgrowth of this structure and of the forces it has generated. . . . The essence of the radical critique is not simply that America is aggressive and imperialistic but that it is so out of an institutional necessity. It is the central assumption that American imperialism must ultimately be traced to the institutional structure of American capitalism that is the common denominator of radical criticism.[38]

American capitalism and the war-making machinery it has generated causes the United States to pose a threat to world peace and prevents social change in many parts of the world. This is what causes "Vietnams," keeps the nuclear arms race going and holds the poor nations down. The real need is for social and economic revolution within the United States so that the United States will pursue a foreign policy of peace and cooperation with all nations of the world.

Underlying this analysis is a belief in the goodness of man. American social and economic structures have corrupted Americans and led to war and repression in the world. Change these structures and man's goodness and the power of ideals will flourish, bringing a world of peace and increasing prosperity.

The more moderate wing of liberal-idealism, represented by writers such as Lester Brown and political figures such as Eugene McCarthy and J. William Fulbright, tends to agree with the new left in seeing America as overly militaristic and, in Vietnam at least, too quick to use military force to prop up a corrupt, dictatorial regime; but it differs from the new left in seeing challenges to peace and equity arising from sources other than just the United States. They do not share the new left's demonological view of American capitalism as virtually the sole cause of world problems. They thereby avoid many of the simplistic tendencies of the new left.[39]

The moderate liberal-idealists are most clearly distinguished, however, by their commitment to international organizations and a belief in the pursuit of international order through international organizations. Fulbright, for example, has declared, "In international as in domestic affairs we are in need of a system of laws rather than of men, a system that does not depend upon the cleverness or benevolence of the men who run it."[40] And Brown has written in a similar vein: "What we must recognize is that the emergence of a global society, which is gradually becoming a technological and historical fact, requires a body of law and the means of enforcing the laws once they are established."[41] In a cautious, yet hopeful, passage Fulbright summarizes the moderate liberal-idealists' basic conviction:

There is very little in international affairs about which I feel certain but there is one thing of which I am quite certain: the necessity of fundamental change in the way nations conduct their relations with each other. It is argued, I am well aware, that an international community to supplant the old system is a hopeless dream. That may be so, but if it is so, the human species has a limited life expectancy. Far therefore from being unrealistic, the dedication of our foreign policy to the single overriding objective of forging the bonds of an international community is not only the course of realism but the only available course of sanity. . . . It is myopic to dismiss the idea of an effective world peace-keeping organization as a visionary ideal, or as anything indeed but an immediate, practical necessity.[42]

Reaction. It is easy for the Christian—with his relatively pessimistic view of man—to mock the liberal-idealists as being hopelessly naive and simple-minded. Their ideas may be all right for discussions in ivory-tower academic circles or in the local garden club, but down in the tough arena of men and power, we all know different rules apply. Although there is much truth in this criticism, I must first pause to give the liberal-idealists credit for their sense of concern, justice and vision. There are dangers in unrealistic visions and simplistic prescriptions, but there are also dangers in unprincipled cynicism and a belief that the status quo is the best man can achieve.

Christianity seeks a balance between a commitment to progress and ideals, and a realization of the imperfections of this world. To ignore the one is as dangerous as to ignore the other. Thus the Christian—mindful of Christ's injunction to love his neighbor as himself and having a vision of government as God's instrument for justice—gives the liberal-idealist credit for his concern over the waste and degradation of war and militarism, for his pursuit of justice and community, and for his efforts to promote human progress and betterment.

But the liberal-idealist position is flawed—so flawed that it has failed in the past and offers no sure guide into the future. In fact, it poses the real danger of adding to our problems.

The root problem with liberal-idealism is its overly optimistic assessment of man's nature, which in turn leads it to misassess the cause of international tensions and problems, to underestimate the intractableness of the world's problems, and to overestimate the speed and ease with which progress can be made. The Christian finds the root cause of international problems in the excessive self-love

169

of man noted in chapter 2. Man is a mixture of good and evil. Corrupted though he is, man sometimes achieves love, goodness and beauty. But it seems that this love, goodness and beauty come to the fore more often in one's personal relations or in relations within one's immediate community or nation than in his relations with the people of other countries.[43] The person who would not be able to bring himself to kill his neighbor, willingly supports his government's wanton killing in some foreign military adventure. The person who donates hours each week in a private welfare agency helping the poor of his city, supports his government's foreign policy which prevents poor nations from raising their standard of living.

In part this callousness may come from ignorance—from a lack of awareness of the full implications of the actions his government is pursuing abroad—for indeed it does take greater effort to discover evils being perpetrated by one's government thousands of miles away than to recognize evils when they are right at one's doorstep. But ignorance is not a full explanation of man's insensitivity to the needs of other peoples and to his own government's working of harm on other peoples. Frequently nations located near each other, sharing many contacts and possessing intimate knowledge of each other, have been extremely antagonistic toward each other's needs and welfare. Cases such as France and Germany prior to the post-World War II era, England and Ireland at various times in history, and Israel and her Arab neighbors today come quickly to mind. Two additional factors are needed to explain why man is more insensitive to the needs of other peoples than to the needs of persons within his immediate community or nation.

The first of these factors is the fact that the nationality, culture, language and racial characteristics which one shares with others in his community and nation make it easier for him to feel responsible for and to identify with them than with others of quite different backgrounds. The differences we saw earlier which tend to separate nations and their peoples is crucial in discouraging the people of one nation from identifying with those of another. To someone thinking in "us" and "them" terms (especially given man's inherent self-love) it becomes easy to ignore "them."

A second additional factor explaining man's insensitivity toward other peoples lies in a strong tendency for man's excessive self-love to become particularly strong and uncritical when it latches onto the national government with which he identifies. Individuals' sense of identification with or feelings of belonging to a nation are helpful to the government of that nation in its exercise of authority and in maintaining its legitimacy. But on the international level they tend to lead to national egoism, as individuals' pride is fed vicariously by the successes and victories of the nation-state with which they identify. Reinhold Niebuhr expressed it this way:

> Unquestionably there is an alloy of projected self-interest in patriotic altruism. The man in the street, with his lust for power and prestige thwarted by his own limitations and the necessities of social life, projects his ego upon his nation and indulges his anarchic lusts vicariously. So the nation is at one and the same time a check upon, and a final vent for, the expression of individual egoism.[44]

The ease with which national leaders all through history have been able to lead their people into wars—wars which wreak pain and havoc on a people as no other governmental policy does—is powerful testimony to the power of self-love when it is transferred to the nation with which one identifies. The leaders of a nation stumble into depression, inflation or other economic dislocations, and the

171

wrath of the people descends upon them; they stumble into a foreign military adventure and the support and help of the people undergirds them.[45] In fact, one long-standing rule of thumb is that if a national leader is confronted by internal dissension, he should start a foreign crisis and then the people will rally behind him.

The net result of all this is a strong predisposition for national governments to act selfishly—to guard their prerogatives jealously and to show a minimal concern for the welfare of other peoples. One ignores this basic fact of political life at his peril.

Yet many of the liberal-idealists' prescriptions for a better world rest on the assumption that governments will voluntarily sacrifice their welfare for the benefit of other peoples. They assume national egoism is an accident of history, not a tendency firmly rooted in human nature. Thus liberal-idealists recommend the internationalization of America's foreign aid program, unilateral disarmament, the rich nations' adopting favorable trade policies toward the poor nations, the giving up of national sovereignty to an international body, and the supporting of anti-western revolutionary movements instead of pro-western established governments.

The root problem with such solutions to international problems is that for them to succeed the very cause of the tensions would have to be eradicated. The point is that we have tensions and problems in the world because of man's, and therefore nations', pride and excessive self-love. Yet for many of the liberal-idealists' solutions to work nations and their citizens would have to put these aside. It is like telling the alcoholic that the cure for his alcoholism is to stop drinking.

In advancing these solutions to world problems liberal-idealists often write in a spirit of "it may not work, but it is the only hope we have." I quoted Fulbright to this effect earlier: "It is argued, I am well aware, that an international community to supplant the old system is a hopeless dream. That may be so, but if it is so, the human species has a limited life expectancy."[46]

Such an approach is an attempt to use pseudo-blackmail to win support for the idealist solution. It poses an absolute dichotomy: Either you accept my solution or the world will be blown to bits by nuclear war, the environment will no longer be able to support life, or some other disaster will descend. Usually the threat is all too real, but often there are solutions other than the liberal-idealist's. But if one accepts the idealist's false dichotomy, he is not likely to search for more immediate, less ideal, but also more attainable solutions (or at least ameliorations). The liberal-idealist thereby diverts attention from the small, yet real, steps mankind might be able to take to improve his lot.

Thus the liberal-idealist—although correctly raising the standard of morality, justice and humane concern—fails to provide us a way out of our morass. His solutions tend to be based on the premise that the cause of our problems no longer exists. The danger is that we will thereby be diverted into pursuing unattainable ideal solutions, while ignoring imperfect, but attainable improvements.

The Conservative-Idealists

Conservative-idealism is in eclipse at the present time, but until just recently it was highly influential in the formation of American foreign policy. It is still held by most of the far right and to some extent by conservative political figures such as Barry Goldwater and George Wallace.

Beliefs. The conservative influence in conservative-idealism is seen in its strong sense of nationalism. A strong pride in the United States and its strength, accomplishments and way of life; an emphasis on the need for strong military forces; and the need for the United States to pursue its national self-interest are all present in conservative-idealism. The idealist influence in conservative-idealism is seen in its acceptance of anticommunism and its support of the American version of democracy and freedom in an absolutistic, moralistic sense. Idealism, as seen earlier, stresses the power of ideals and rationality in international relations, but under the impact of conservatism's nationalism this emphasis is transformed into a belief in the ideal of the American way of life and in anticommunism. This ideal is then impregnated with the missionary fervor of moralism to which idealism is prone. It is seen as a moral absolute: Communism is to be opposed wherever it rears its ugly head and Americanism is to be defended at all costs. In the process national self-interest sometimes is forced to take a back seat to the moral crusade of anticommunism.

The commitment of the conservative-idealist to a strident anticommunist, proAmerican attitude in practice leads him to eschew trade with communist countries, which could be mutually beneficial; to risk war, with all of its staggering costs, in order to "liberate" communist countries; to attack compromise treaty arrangements and other forms of international cooperation which could benefit the United States as selling out to the enemy. While the liberal-idealist is willing to sacrifice national self-interest in support of international order or world disarmament, the conservative-idealist is willing to sacrifice national self-interest in support of the ideal of anticommunism.

Barry Goldwater, for example, has reflected some of these characteristics. In Goldwater's view the United States and communism are in a struggle to the death; either one or the other will prevail. He wrote in 1960 that our national leadership over the past fourteen years has favored neither surrender nor treason. It is equally clear, however, that our leaders have not made *victory* the goal of American policy. . . .

We want a peace in which freedom and justice will prevail, and that—given the nature of Communism— is a peace in which Soviet power will no longer be in a position to threaten us and the rest of the world. A tolerable peace, in other words, must *follow* victory over Communism.[47]

Goldwater opposed negotiations and cultural exchange programs with the Soviet Union and questioned the value of the United Nations.[48] The United States is blameless: "The only 'tensions' that exist between East and West have been created, and deliberately so, by the Communists."[49]

This same sort of anticommunist zeal is reflected in George Wallace's 1971 criticism of Richard Nixon's trip to China as a "colossal mistake" and a "disaster," comparable to Neville Chamberlain's trip to Munich where he compromised away the independence of Czechoslovakia and on the same order as a trip by Roosevelt to Berlin to negotiate with Hitler would have been.[50]

The writings and statements of the far right spokesmen are replete with nationalistic pride and anticommunist fervor. A war is going on between the United States and communism—a war the United States is losing.

The cold war is real war. It has already claimed more lives, enslaved more people, and cost more money than any "hot" war in history. Yet, most Americans refuse to admit that we are at war. That is why we are rapidly losing—why America has yet to win its first real victory in 18 years of "cold" war.[51]

Strong military forces and a willingness to use them are indispensable to victory in that war. Anticommunist crusader Billy James Hargis raises the question, "Should we surrender to Castro or SMASH him?" His answer: "Truth demands the liquidation of Fidel Castro. Honor demands the liberation of Cuba from the hands of this godless despot."[52]

Reaction. Many of the conservative-idealists, especially those of the far right, attempt to tie in their anticommunism, Americanism ideal with Christianity. Billy James Hargis, for example, has written,

Communism is not a political party as such. It is a ruthless movement dedicated to the destruction of Christianity. The only sure way to stamp out Communism and its ideas is through the Word of God. Communism cannot survive in a truly Christian nation. Remember, there is no freedom without God.[53]

Thus one might suppose Christianity offers support to the anticommunism and nationalism of the conservative-idealists. But this is not so. Earlier I showed that nationalism in an extreme, uncritical form is contrary to Christian values.[54] Concern and love for nation is to be balanced by concern and love for all men, regardless of nationality. Wedding a fervent anticommunism to a strong nationalism, as the conservative-idealists do, leads to an even worse commitment. Senator Mark Hatfield has clearly made the needed points:

Far Righters often equate Communism with the devil and America with God. And God, to the Far Righters, is a personification of a white, Protestant, anti-Communist American. They have turned the scriptural tables and created God in their image.

This unholy marriage of religion and politics has produced a perverted Christianity based not on love but hate, not on charity but persecution. The Far Righters are definitely not practicing religious fundamentalism, as they claim, but are actually practicing a form of paganism. They worship at the idol of "country" and have substituted the gospel of anti-Communism for the gospel of Christ.[55]

Hatfield has placed his finger on the two key errors of the conservative-idealists. First, their praise of the United States and pride in its past accomplishments are much too uncritical and undiscriminating. Christianity offers standards by which one's nation can be judged and evaluated. "Test the spirits to see whether they are of God,"[56] the apostle John admonished the early Christians, and we should do no less. But the nationalism of the conservative-idealists blindly asserts the goodness and purity of the United States, and thereby ignores the prophetic tradition of Christianity—such as is seen in Jesus Christ and the Old Testament prophets—which critically evaluates and passes judgment on social-political structures. To assume the near-perfect goodness of one's own nation is implicitly to deny the imperfections of man's nature—for if all men (including Americans) are marred by sin, the social-political structures of any human society (including the American) are bound to be less than perfect and in need of improvement.

The second basic error of the conservative-idealist—to which Hatfield also makes reference—is the tendency to see communism as the supreme evil and thereby anti-communism as the supreme good. This is moralism. Christianity teaches that evil is too broad and too pervasive in human affairs to be monopolized by one social-political movement. Surely Christianity recognizes the evils of communism; they are real and formidable. But the evils of colonialism, materialism and fascist-type authoritarianism are also real and formidable. To elevate communism to the supreme evil in the world is just too simplistic. The real world is more complex—and more evil—than that. If all evil were concentrated in one movement, a Christian's task of making the world a better place to live would be greatly simplified. Christianity opposes communism, but

177

it also opposes colonialism, materialism, fascism and all other movements or value systems which deny the true nature of man and God's will for man.

The Conservative-Realists

Conservative-realism has long vied with both liberal- and conservative-idealism over the proper approach to foreign policy making. With the fading of liberal-idealism since World War II and the more recent eclipse of the fervent anticommunism of conservative-idealism, both forms of realism, but especially conservative-realism, have been growing in ascendancy. This trend is being aided by the fact that many view the error of American involvement in Vietnam to be a case of misplaced idealism and by the fact that Richard Nixon is basically a conservative-realist.

Beliefs. Conservative-realism can perhaps best be described as the purest form of realism. It is realism undiluted by considerations of moral obligations or principles. Thus it accepts all the chief tenets of realism discussed earlier: the propensity of man toward evil, the efficacy in international politics of coercive power (and the weakness of ideals), and the defense of the national interest as the highest priority. Through a process of negotiation and bargaining, national power is used to create a balance or equilibrium of power in the world which, in turn, leads to stability on the international scene. Conservatism, with its strong nationalistic emphasis, strengthens realism's emphasis on national self-interest. Conservatism also adds a national pride and fervor which give conservatism-realism an even greater emphasis on national self-interest and pushes considerations of moral principles even further into the background.

Richard Nixon revealed his strong nationalistic tendencies in his 1972 State of the Union address:

And as we look back over this century, let us, in the highest spirit of bipartisanship, recognize that we can be proud of our nation's record in foreign affairs.

America has given more generously of itself towards maintaining freedom, preserving peace, and alleviating human suffering around the globe, than any nation has ever done in the history of man.

We have fought four wars in this century, but our power has never been used to break the peace, only to keep it; never been used to destroy freedom, only to defend it.[57]

But these nationalistic tendencies of Nixon did not lead, in his thinking, to an aggressive foreign policy, motivated by a militant anticommunism, as it does in the case of conservative-idealists. Instead Nixon's realism led him to a determination to defend what he rather narrowly defined as American interests. This is seen in another statement Nixon made in his 1972 State of the Union address:

We will act to defend our interests, whenever and wherever they are threatened any place in the world. But where our interests or our treaty commitments are not involved, our role will be limited.[58]

Nixon's willingness to enter into diplomatic contacts with China and to initiate massive trade programs with both the Soviet Union and China revealed in practice a willingness to put national self-interests ahead of ideological purity. (The trade with the Soviet Union and China helped greatly in meeting the United States' balance-of-payments problems.) In 1970, Nixon explicitly called for a foreign policy based on self-interest and not on ideals:

Our negotiations on strategic arms limitations and in other areas will have far greater chance of success if both sides enter them motivated by mutual self-interest rather than naive sentimentality.

It is with this same spirit that we have resumed dis-

179

cussions with Communist China in our talks at Warsaw.[59]

Hans Morgenthau has been the most prominent scholar supporting a conservative-realist position. Although his position is not marked by the sense of nationalistic pride which characterizes Nixon's, yet he can best be considered in the conservative-realist camp because his realism remains basically untempered by considerations of moral principle or obligation. Morgenthau explicitly excludes questions of legality and morality from political decision making:

> The lawyer asks: "Is this policy in accord with the rules of law?" The moralist asks: "Is this policy in accord with moral principles?" And the political realist asks: "How does this policy affect the power of the nation?" . . .
>
> The political realist is not unaware of the existence and relevance of a standard of thought other than the political one. As political realist, he cannot but subordinate these other standards to the political one. And he parts company with other schools when they impose standards of thought appropriate to other spheres upon the political one.[60]

This amoral position, however, leads to justice: "For if we look at all nations, our own included, as political entities pursuing their respective interests defined in terms of power, we are able to do justice to all of them."[61] Justice emerges out of each nation pursuing its own self-interest apart from any moral considerations.

Conservative-realists see American problems in Vietnam as the result of becoming lost in the conservative-idealist anticommunist mania instead of following national self-interest.[62] If only, the argument goes, the United States had followed its national interests it would have seen that its interests in the outcome of a guerrilla war in a small Asian nation thousands of miles from its shores has

180

no significant relationship to its national interest. Thus whether or not the United States should intervene in other limited wars depends upon whether or not vital American interests are at stake. Since conservative-realists tend to define national interest in fairly constricted terms, the answer will usually be no. The way to avoid war is to maintain a strong military deterrent and then negotiate from a position of strength.

Thus conservative-realism ought not to be interpreted as a form of isolationism, as a fortress America mentality. The United States is to be active in the world political arena, defending its interest and seeking to maintain a stable world order through the creation of an equilibrium among the world powers—all the time negotiating and bargaining to achieve these ends. Nixon's policy of detente with the Soviet Union and China ought to be seen in this light. Detente is made possible by the American decision that repression and injustices within the Soviet Union or China ought not to stand in the way of negotiations and cooperation. American self-interest, not the morality of cooperating with repressive regimes, should be the guiding principle. The way is then opened for detente to play the key role in an attempt to reach world peace by creating an equilibrium of power among the United States, the Soviet Union and China. And that equilibrium is to be maintained through negotiations, high-level diplomacy, trade and other contacts.

Reaction. Conservative-realism correctly recognizes the imperfections in man and human affairs. This saves conservative-realists from the naivete of the liberal-idealists and the moralistic anticommunism of the conservative-idealists. Especially conservative-realism's repudiation of moralism (the absolutizing of a moral principle so as to make it rigidly applicable in all circumstances) is an advance and no doubt helps safeguard against a promiscuous interventionism.

But the problem with conservative-realism is that, while avoiding the trap of moral absolutism, it falls into the trap of moral irrelevancy. To apply moral principles in an absolutistic fashion is disastrous; to declare moral principles irrelevant is equally disastrous. As I suggested earlier and as I will argue more fully in the next section, to reject the applicability of moral principles to foreign policy issues is to deny that one owes anything to a neighbor who lives across a political boundary. Neither respect, nor rights, nor life, nor help is due him. This Christianity rejects. Man is of infinite worth, and respect, rights, life and help are due him because he is a man, made in God's image. And one's obligation to give his fellow man his due does not stop just because he lives under the jurisdiction of another government. Conservative-realism's denial of this basic point becomes especially serious when we remember that the pursuit of national interest often will not be merely neutral in its effects on other peoples, but will cause them harm.

Conservative-realists like to pose a dichotomy between moral absolutism and moral irrelevancy and then force us to choose between them.[63] But this is a false dichotomy. There are other alternatives, as the liberal-realists have shown, and as I will show later.

Conservative-realists complain that the anticommunism of conservative-idealists got the United States into the Vietnam quagmire, but surely part of the blame must also be borne by the conservative-realists, with their amoral approach to foreign policy. It would have been impossible for men with sensitive moral consciences to have justified the kill ratios, "pacification" programs, free fire zones, and lies of Vietnam. But conservative-realists had told us that "moral man" is to be held separate from "political man."[64] With morals divorced from politics,

Vietnam becomes easily understandable. Declaring moral principles irrelevant and bowing down to the idol of national self-interest, Americans found it was easy to convince themselves that the United States' self-interest indeed did require stopping the Viet Cong. The "domino theory" and declaring Vietnam to be a test case for wars of national liberation were means to demonstrate American self-interest in Vietnam. Admittedly, the anticommunism of conservative-idealism played a role by clouding the decision-makers' judgment of what was and what was not in the national interest, but conservative-realists' advocating that national self-interest, apart from moral considerations, should be the sole norm of American foreign policy made possible the final tragedy of American involvement.

Finally, the sense of national pride which afflicts conservative-realists is no more defensible when it becomes excessive than is excessive self-love in an individual. When the President of the United States seeks to justify a policy on the basis that he does not want the United States to "become a second-rate power and to see this nation accept the first defeat in its proud 190-year history,"[65] then national self-love has indeed become excessive. And conservative-realism is no defense against that.

The Liberal-Realists

The resurgence of realism in the post-World War II years led to a growth in influence of liberal-realism, as well as conservative-realism. Most of the prominent figures in the liberal or moderate wings of both political parties—men such as Edward Kennedy, George McGovern, Edmund Muskie and Charles Percy—fall into the liberal-realist camp. They are foreign policy realists, but their political liberalism has tempered their realism. Other than elected figures, men such as Reinhold Niebuhr, George Kennan and Henry Kissinger are among the more prominent liberal-realists.

Beliefs. The joining of liberalism and realism appears to be a joining of opposites: Liberalism believes in the goodness of man, realism in the inherent imperfections of man; liberalism believes in the likelihood of progress, realism in the difficulties of progress; liberalism believes in the need to commit American foreign policy to justice and freedom, realism in the need to commit American foreign policy to the defense of national self-interest. Yet the persons cited above have, with somewhat different emphases, combined aspects of both the realist and liberal outlooks so that their foreign policy is informed by both.

These liberal-realists typically accept realism's view of the efficacy of coercive power (and the weakness of ideals) in international politics and also accept national self-interest as a proper goal of foreign policy. In this sense they are realists. Yet their realism is modified by the impact of liberalism's concern for morality in foreign policy—for having not only national self-interest but also freedom and justice for all men as foreign policy goals. The realism of some liberal-realists has also been modified by liberalism's optimistic view of man and belief in progress.

Regarding the modification of realism by a concern for morality in foreign policy, the liberal-realist does not see national self-interest as the one and only goal of foreign policy. The conservative-realists' harshness and lack of concern toward human needs and suffering bothers the liberal-realists. In the process the concept of national self-interest as the single goal of one's foreign policy is modified. National self-interest is important, but moral considerations demand that other factors also be taken into account.

Reinhold Niebuhr took this position when he wrote that "nations must use their power with the purpose of making

it an instrument of justice and a servant of interests broader than their own."[66] He explicitly criticized an overly
nationalistic conception of the national interest, since
"egotism is not the proper cure for an abstract and pre-
tentious idealism."[67] Yet Niebuhr's realism is clearly seen
in his belief in the need for power to back up ideals and
rationality; they are not their own defense as the idealists
would have it.

> Some balance of power is the basis of whatever justice
> is achieved in human relations. Where the dispropor-
> tion of power is too great and where an equilibrium
> of social forces is lacking, no mere rational or moral de-
> mands can achieve justice.[68]

Liberal-realists such as Niebuhr tend to see the national
interest as a more complex concept than do conservative-
realists. They argue against defining the national self-
interest in too narrow or too immediate a form. Pursuing
justice and morality is, they often argue, in the long run
more in the national interest than pursuing one's immediate, narrowly defined self-interest. Niebuhr once wrote,

> But a consistent self-interest on the part of a nation will
> work against its interests because it will fail to do justice
> to the broader and longer interests, which are involved
> with the interests of other nations. A narrow national
> loyalty on our part, for instance, will obscure our long
> range interests where they are involved with those of a
> whole alliance of free nations. Thus the loyalty of a leav-
> ening portion of a nation's citizens to a value trans-
> cending national interest will save a realistic nation
> from defining its interests in such narrow and short
> range terms as to defeat the real interests of the nation.[69]

And Senator Edward Kennedy once revealed this same
type of thinking:

> We must, then, understand our own interest in pro-
> viding foreign aid. In addition to strengthening the

security of nations, its key role is to contribute to the peace of the world, by accelerating development along peaceful paths in the poor half of the world.[70]

Henry Kissinger and George Kennan, two persons whose careers have spanned both the practice and academic analysis of foreign policy making, also typify the liberal-realist belief that moral considerations should temper national-interest considerations (although they are probably somewhat closer to the conservative-realist position than is Niebuhr). Kissinger, for example, has argued that a balance between power-politics' pursuit of self-interest and moral purpose must be maintained:

The dilemma is that there can be no stability without equilibrium but, equally, equilibrium is not a purpose with which we can respond to the travail of our world. ... A clearer understanding of America's interests and of the requirements of equilibrium can give perspective to our idealism and lead to humane and moderate objectives, especially in relation to political and social change. Thus our conception of world order must have deeper purposes than stability but greater restraints on our behavior than would result if it were approached only in a fit of enthusiasm.[71]

And Kennan, while upholding the realist position, once went so far as to write, in discussing the horrors of weapons of mass destruction, that

I am skeptical of the meaning of the terms "victory" and "defeat" in their relation to modern war between great countries. To my mind, the defeat is war itself. In any case it seems that there are times when we have no choice but to follow the dictates of our conscience, to throw ourselves on God's mercy, and not to ask too many questions.[72]

Later in the same article Kennan discussed environmental pollution and overpopulation within a framework of moral values beyond the mere pursuit of national self-interest.

The liberal-realist is thereby pretty much a complete realist in taking a hard-nosed stand in defense of the need for power politics and a balance of power to affect and change the world political arena. Yet his moral concerns and tendencies toward optimism sometimes lead him to use power politics in causes in which he believes justice and morality demand actions, but which the conservative-realist would avoid.

Thus in questions of war and peace the liberal-realists share many of the foreign policy positions of the conservative-realists. Both stress the need for a believable military deterrence, leading to a balance of power, as the best way to peace in an imperfect world. The greater willingness of the liberal-realists to give weight to humane considerations leads them to be less comfortable with a balance of nuclear terror, and more often than the conservative-realists they call for negotiations to reduce nuclear armaments.

The approach of the liberal-realists to issues of injustice and repression in the world typifies the liberal-realist tendency to introduce moral considerations by taking a broad, long-term view of American self-interest. They often conclude that opposing injustices is in the long-term American interest. Thus a more humane, justice-seeking element tempers what in the conservative-realist position tends to be coldness.

Some liberal-realists, seeing human nature in a more optimistic light than realism does and therefore being more optimistic about the likelihood of progress in international affairs, edge closer to liberal-idealism than do Niebuhr, Kissinger and Kennan. Edward Kennedy, for example, has given evidence of an underlying optimism and a readiness to consider ideals and moral dimensions in foreign policy questions, while still not relinquishing a realist's belief in the need to defend the national interest with coercive power when necessary. He once wrote,

> In the field of foreign policy, our primary aims during the 1970s should be to try to end the cold war that has dominated world politics for the past twenty years, and to help bring about economic progress in the poor nations. Based on the changes that have taken place in recent years, and the forces in motion in the world, I think there is a good chance to accomplish these ends without endangering our own national interests.[73]

A drive to better the world and a feeling of optimism that it can be done is mentioned in the same breath as the protection of the national interest.

Later Kennedy revealed a basic commitment to the value of military force when he wrote concerning NATO, "It gave the Soviets a very real risk to balance before starting an invasion. It has helped to keep the peace for over fifteen years."[74]

In short, the liberal-realists, although encompassing several shadings of points of view, are agreed on the need to defend the national interest and to use coercive power in pursuit of foreign policy goals, and on the need to augment a crass concern for national interest with more humane considerations of justice and morality.

Reaction. There is much in liberal-realism to commend it. Its relatively pessimistic view of man and resulting view of coercive power as a necessary tool in international politics save it from the mistaken, and sometimes naive, conclusions that liberal-idealism often falls into. Yet its moral concerns save it from the amoral cynicism of the conservative-realists. And both its realism and its moral concerns save it from the anticommunist zealotry of the conservative-idealists.

Clearly liberal-realism is superior to the other three basic approaches to foreign policy formation with which it is vying for domination in the United States. It builds on an accurate appraisal of the nature of man and adds a sense of moral concern. The balance of the two gives one realism without cynicism, idealism without illusions.

But there are problems with liberal-realism, problems so severe that it has not yet given the sort of direction and purpose to American foreign policy that it is potentially capable of giving. The key source of these problems is a great deal of fuzziness when it comes to the content of the moral principles to be applied to the formation of foreign policy. When liberal-realists speak of the need for moral considerations they usually seem to have in mind some sort of general humanitarian values, usually derived from the broad Judeo-Christian ethic. This is, of course, not all bad by any means. Better to have values such as these than the amoralism of the conservative-realists.

But this lack of precision does lead to real problems. Political issues are highly complex, involving multi-faceted factual and historical elements and morally ambiguous situations. Often moral values clash and the facts themselves will be unclear. In such a situation a fuzzy framework of values cannot give the direction which is needed. Tough choices must be made, but there are no tough criteria by which to make them. As a result moral principles become sort of a genie in a bottle—to be called upon and used when and how desired. Moral principles can be found to support almost any conclusion.

What is needed is a well-marked-out, self-consciously held framework of values. Only with such a moral perspective can one realistically hope to cut through the moral dilemmas of foreign policy making and point out a better way. Yet most liberal-realists seem content with a very general, vague moral code, with the result that the values of liberal-realism can be made to serve almost any master. This may well be the chief reason why the liberal-

189

realists were as ineffectual as they were in opposing the Vietnam War and were divided on the basic issues of American military involvement.

While the formation of a precise, sophisticated framework of moral principles with which to evaluate and formulate foreign policies is beyond the scope of this book (and perhaps beyond the scope of mortal man), in the next chapter I set out what I believe the values and insights of evangelical Christianity suggest should be some of the chief concepts of such a framework. It is to that task we now turn.

7
Progressive Realism: A New Option in International Politics

IT TAKES NEITHER A GREAT PROPHET nor a confirmed pessimist to foresee an increasingly dangerous world in the latter decades of the twentieth century. Weapons of mass destruction and unlimited capabilities for limited wars, when combined with threatening environmental disaster and economic interdependence, create a mixture which is indeed filled with explosive potential. The alternative approaches to foreign policy making outlined earlier do not have the answers for modern man. Worldwide turmoil and continuing injustices at best and nuclear or ecological devastation at worst appear to be the prognosis. It is hard to be optimistic. Man is unleashing forces which neither his nature nor his international institutions seem capable of handling.

Earlier we noted the gravity of the United States' domestic problems. Grave as they are, there is yet hope that politics may stave off disaster. Government is at least a tool which, if used properly, could do much to alleviate our most pressing problems. But on the international scene there is no comparable tool. To prescribe essentially political solutions in an apolitical arena is not helpful. To be helpful at all one must give due weight to the nature of both the problems confronting the world and the means available to meet them.

If we must avoid neat, set answers to domestic problems (as I urged we must in prior chapters) we must surely avoid them in dealing with international issues. The difficulties are too great, the future too uncertain, the moral ambiguities too frequent, and man's judgments too susceptible to self-delusion and error, to do otherwise. Thus what I attempt to set out in this section is neither a comprehensive answer to the United States' foreign policy challenges nor the only approach in keeping with Christian values and insights. Instead I set out some of the basic ingredients of a foreign policy approach which I believe are consistent with Christian values and insights. Even with their inherent limitations—limitations which I readily acknowledge—they advance us beyond the naivete of the liberal-idealists, the nationalistic fervor of the conservative-idealists, the amoralism and cynicism of the conservative-realists and the uncertain standards of the liberal-realists.

Just as in domestic affairs, progressive realism in international affairs seeks to build upon a well-thought-out conception of the nature and purposes of both man and politics, and from them to reach out to the world around with a realistic assessment of both the limitations and potentials of man and politics. It thereby seeks a realistic balance between the possibilities and the difficulties of progress. It seeks to avoid both a naive optimism and a cynical despair, both a cold commitment to a narrow national self-interest and a paternalistic, morally arrogant interventionism. It seeks a better way.

FIVE BASIC INGREDIENTS OF A BETTER WAY
The basic ingredients of that better way can be summarized under five headings. These ingredients do not constitute a political program. Rather they are elements crucial to a new option in a progressive, yet realistic, foreign policy.

Coercive Power as the Basic Force
The first of these basic ingredients is the view that the world political arena is a tough arena, where coercive power counts more than good intentions and virtue. Here one finds much of the realism in progressive realism. As discussed earlier, evangelical Christianity rejects the idealists' belief in the power of ideals and virtue in the international arena. Man's evil nature is too intractable and the temptation to slip into a blind nationalism too great to allow even the level of selflessness and concern for others found on the personal level to be reached on the international level. National leaders are encouraged by both their own natures and their populaces to take a stance favoring the immediate self-interest of their nation—even at the expense of other peoples. Man's nature, in short, leads nations to act in an exploitive, acquisitive manner.

Thus coercive power, especially military and economic in nature, and not feelings of obligation and loyalty to abstract ideals necessarily remain the basic factor by which nations exert their wills in world affairs. Since each nation is committed to pursuing its own self-interest, only force— force which is able to threaten severe sanctions or promise bright rewards—is able to move a nation from its intended course of action. The picture is not very pretty, but it is accurate. Pretending it is otherwise guarantees failure from the start.

The belief that this situation will change and that some sort of world government, based upon worldwide acceptance of its authority, may emerge in the foreseeable future is not realistic. The difficulty with attaining a true world government is the essentially organic nature of government pointed out in chapter 3. What makes government what it is, is the authority conferred upon it by its citizens through their accepting its legitimacy. Government, at heart, rests upon learned, internalized attitudes and habits, not upon laws and legally created institutions.

For a world government to be possible, almost all persons throughout the world would have to be socialized into accepting its authority—obviously a prospect not likely to materialize in the foreseeable future. National loyalties are too deeply ingrained for that. Here we are again confronted by the tendency for man's excessive self-love to be translated into excessive love for the nation or for some other linguistic, national, religious or ethnic group with which he identifies. It is fairly easy for man's self-love to manifest itself in love for an immediate group with which one identifies, such as a family, village or tribe. But as the unit with which we wish the individual to identify becomes larger it becomes more difficult to maintain that sense of loyalty and identity essential for effective government. To ask man to sacrifice his own desires and pleasures for the good of larger and larger units is to ask him to go against his own innate self-love. To expect these sorts of feelings to develop worldwide—overcoming tremendous national, cultural and religious barriers—is totally unrealistic.

Nevertheless certain forms of institutionalized international cooperation are possible. The Universal Postal Union and the International Telecommunications Union, while not governments, are examples of institutionalized international cooperation. Governments have banded together for certain purposes, and the organizational structures they have created have acquired a regular pattern of interaction and a certain life of their own. More could be done with organizations of this type. They could go a step beyond what has been done thus far and seek to impose coercive sanctions upon governments—even nonmember governments—who refuse to abide by their decisions. This could be a recourse in the area of pollution. The success of such efforts would depend upon the relative strength and will of the nations imposing the sanctions and the nation being sanctioned, although some have questioned the morality of such actions. The United Nations has attempted such actions in regard to Southern Rhodesia after it unilaterally declared its independence from Britain and South Africa in opposition to its apartheid policies—both without notable success, it might be added. Yet such institutionalized international cooperation and even imposition of sanctions remains a potential tool of international politics. Although the successful building up of such organizations is fraught with difficulties, to do so at least does not run counter to innate human nature nor to the nature of international politics.

In summary, coercive power remains the basic force in international politics, and world government a visionary illusion with no realistic chance of success in the foreseeable future. Some limited forms of regularized, institutionalized international cooperation are, however, possible.

The Possibility of Progress

The second element basic to the progressive-realist approach to world politics is the belief that progress in international affairs is possible. Although I have painted a bleak picture of the nature of international politics, this does not mean that the picture is one of unalterable, un-

195

changing bleakness. Some periods of time are marked by relative stability, peace and mutually beneficial actions by nations; other periods by instability, war and actions destructive of national interests. This fact is obvious. Its implications should be equally obvious: Progress (as well of course as regression) in international affairs is possible. There are certain conditions and actions which lead to a more secure, more prosperous world and other conditions and actions which lead to a less secure, less prosperous world. The differences are great enough to warrant major efforts to discover and seek out those conditions and actions which lead to progress and to avoid those which lead to regression and decay. Progress is difficult. It is a difficult, rocky climb, and catastrophes which would wipe out all progress constantly threaten; yet progress can be made. The world can be made a safer, saner home for man, and that makes all the efforts worthwhile. The marriage of realism and progressivism—of a hard-nosed, no-nonsense view of the world and of a belief in the possibility of improvement—is at the core of the Christian view of international politics I have called *progressive realism*. (And it is also at the core of the progressive-realist view of domestic policies, as I stressed in the prior chapter.)

The Relevance of Moral Principles
The third element basic to progressive realism is a belief that foreign policy decisions must be informed by moral principles. It rejects the contention of most realists that moral principles may be fine in our individual, personal lives, but do not apply—or at least apply in a different way —in the making of foreign policy. Honesty, charity, selflessness may be all right for an individual in his personal life, but not for an individual in his role as a foreign policymaker. This a Christian rejects. Moral principles are just as important and as controlling in one's decisions as a foreign

196

policy-maker as they are in one's decisions as a parent or ordinary citizen.

What must be clearly understood, however, is that acting morally, either in private or in public life, is not a matter of taking one or two moral principles and applying them in any and all circumstances in a simplistic, dogmatic fashion (as many realists imply is the case).[1] Most situations are morally ambiguous, marked by clashing moral principles and values. Moral choices are never easy. This is true of the father, for example, who, in choosing whether to spend more time with his family or in community service, must sort out competing moral responsibilities. He has a moral obligation to both and he must seek the proper balance. The foreign policy-maker faces morally similar situations. He has responsibilities to his own nation and its people. This is a basic moral responsibility. But the foreign policy-maker also has responsibilities toward other peoples and their governments. (I suggest shortly what some of these moral responsibilities are.) Thus often the decision-maker will find himself in morally ambiguous situations, situations in which he has to sort out conflicting moral principles and determine which—on the basis of available information and relevant criteria— ought to take precedence and what sort of a balance to strike. For the foreign policy-maker, especially those in powerful positions in major world powers such as the United States, the stakes in terms of world affairs are much higher than they are for most of us in our personal lives. Yet the same basic moral principles apply: Christianity admits of no double standard of morality.

The Basic Purpose of Foreign Policy

I am convinced that much of the uncertainty and fogginess about the basic goal of American foreign policy can be traced back to a tendency to view the purposes of foreign policy in isolation from the purposes of domestic policies. The two are often seen as separate, distinct areas with two separate, distinct purposes. But government is basically one and its God-given purpose for existing is basically one.

Thus to think clearly about foreign policy purposes one must start with the basic purpose of government generally, not with some supposed basic purpose of government as a foreign policy actor. In chapter 3 I argued that the basic purpose God intends for government consists of the establishment of just order—one which maximizes man's true personal freedom, that is, man's opportunities to develop and exercise his creative capacities in keeping with God's law of love.[2] This pursuit of a just order should play as central a role in informing a nation's foreign policies as it does in informing a nation's domestic policies.

In chapters 3 and 4 I argued that innumerable forces within a nation threaten man's freedom and the existence of opportunities for a creative, satisfying life. It is the purpose of government to so control and regulate these forces that an order marked by justice—by a maximization of true freedom—is achieved. But there are also justice-destroying forces of an international or nondomestic nature which threaten man's freedom and creative opportunities. Foreign conquest which imposes a repressive, freedom-denying government upon a people is the clearest example of a nondomestic force denying freedom. But foreign forces can also deny freedom by subtler means. Trade and monetary policies of one government which impoverish another or result in severe economic dislocations is a particularly clear example. Thousands of workers can be thrown out of work and denied the opportunity to support themselves and their families by a decision of another government thousands of miles away.

Just as it is the responsibility of the American government to protect its citizens from the freedom-denying effects of domestic forces, so also it is its responsibility to protect them from the freedom-denying effects of non-domestic forces. Americans' freedom of action is threatened by foreign military forces, by the polluting action of other nations which are threatening the United States with ecological disaster, and, in an increasingly interdependent world, by trade and monetary policies of other nations and multinational corporations. To stave off these threatened injustices and to maximize Americans' creative opportunities is a primary responsibility of the American government. The basic purpose of government in the Christian view is to provide order, justice and freedom to the citizens under its jurisdiction, not to serve as a worldwide judge and policeman. Its primary responsibility is to its citizens, not to the citizens under the jurisdiction of other governments.

In some ways this emphasis on protecting the freedom of one's own citizens sounds like the realists' emphasis on national self-interest, and progressive realism indeed emphasizes one's own nation and its people's needs. But my position here is distinguishable from that of the realists' position in that, first, the realists—and this is especially true of the conservative-realists—usually do not clearly define national self-interest, with the result that it tends to slip into nationalism and power for power's sake. Anything which builds up the prestige, power and economic or military might of the nation is seen as being in the national self-interest. My position here—to the extent it can be considered a national self-interest position—defines that self-interest in very restricted terms. It is not the nation as such which is to be defended—which, with its semimystical connotations, all too easily produces an overly nationalistic power-for-power's-sake syndrome. Instead my position argues that it is the freedom of individual citizens that is to be protected and maximized. The individual and his creative freedom is the focus, not the mystical entity of the nation.

But there is a second, even more basic way in which my position here is distinguishable from that of national self-interest. The prime responsibility of foreign policy-makers toward the citizens of their own country is one half of a dual responsibility. The other half is to act toward other countries with justice—to give them their due as countries. But what is their due? I would suggest that it is so to act toward them that they are not hindered in fulfilling the purpose they ought to be fulfilling for their citizens. This purpose, in turn, is to protect and maximize the true freedom of their citizens. Every government, in the Christian view, has the duty to maximize and protect the true freedom of its citizens and the creative opportunities and reaching of full humanity which goes with that freedom. Each nation should conduct its foreign policy with that purpose in mind, but in doing so it must remember that every other government has that same responsibility toward its people. Each government has a right to be able to pursue that purpose without hindrance from other governments; each government, therefore, has an obligation to so conduct its foreign policy that it does not hinder other governments in the performance of their purpose. The key element, therefore, is the basic purpose God has given governments, and it is that which must be used as a guiding, discriminating factor. It is that which usually is forgotten in foreign policy discussions and decisions.

It should be noted that this responsibility which one government has toward another—although real and significant—is limited. It is based on justice, on giving that government its due, on respecting its rights as a government, not on vaguer, less discriminating concepts of humanitarianism or international brotherhood. Thus the American government has a very real, but also a very limited, responsibility toward other nations. Progressive realism is thereby distinguished from conservative-realism in that it seeks a standard based on a sense of morality and justice; it is distinguished from liberal-realism in that it seeks a sharply formulated standard rather than simply a commitment to more general moral principles.

In saying this I do not mean to imply that this standard can be easily and simply applied. Often the decision-maker will have to balance his responsibility to safeguard the freedom of the citizens of his country against his responsibility not to hinder other governments from safeguarding the freedom of their citizens. In the area of trade policies, for example, the decision-maker has a responsibility to protect economic opportunities and stability within his country, but he also has a responsibility not to use the economic power of his country to plunder and wreck the economy of some other nation, rendering it impossible for that country's government to provide the economic stability and opportunities necessary for the development and freedom of its citizens. Although his responsibilities on balance will often be clear, there will also sometimes be gray areas where honest men will disagree on which responsibility the situation indicates should take precedence. But the important point to remember is that a decision-maker does have a responsibility toward other nations, yet it is a limited responsibility, one based on a sense of justice which respects that government's rights.

This dual standard, I am suggesting, is the basic purpose of foreign policy and ought to form the basis of American foreign policy. Although these two goals appear simple and perhaps even self-evident, if consistently applied they would remake American foreign policy. Goals such as this would have challenged American attempts to prop up a succession of apparently corrupt, undemocratic

201

governments in South Vietnam from 1954 to 1973. Although American honor as some sort of a mystical entity and although maybe a nationalistic anticommunist fervor would call for such support, the goal of protecting the American people's freedom would not. The freedom-limiting aspects of the draft, the death and suffering to American men and their families, and the huge military expenditures far outweighed any remote safeguarding of a just political order which enables Americans to be more free.

Such goals as I am proposing here would condemn the trade policies the United States and most of the industrialized countries follow toward the poor, largely agricultural countries, policies which erect barriers against the importation of goods produced by these countries and result in millions in these countries being jobless.[3] The rich countries, including the United States, obviously have a responsibility to their own people which includes protecting them from economic disadvantages and hardships. But when a super-rich country such as the United States follows trade policies which make it virtually impossible for other nations and their governments to develop strong, viable economies which can provide their citizens with the steady employment and decent wages necessary for a full, creative life, the United States is in the wrong. Both values, both responsibilities, must be recognized. Under the impact of realism, only the responsibilities to one's own people and nation—however defined—are recognized.

The Right of Intervention

These first four ingredients of the progressive-realist approach to foreign policy making leave a troublesome question unanswered: Does the United States ever have a right to involve itself and intervene in international disputes or other nations' domestic affairs, even when neither protecting the freedom of United States' citizens nor justice to other nations (as defined in the prior section) demand it?

On the one hand, this question could be answered with a no. First, there is the ever-present danger that American intervention will degenerate into a promiscuous interventionism. Few persons support a world policeman's role for the United States in which it seeks to right all the wrongs it finds. Yet on specific issues—from the Soviet Union's treatment of its Jewish citizens to South Africa's treatment of its black citizens, from Britain's treatment of Northern Ireland to the torture of political prisoners by an authoritarian Brazilian government, from Portugal's treatment of its African colonies to Pakistan's treatment of East Pakistan (now Bangla Desh)—there is no lack of voices calling for American action to correct perceived wrongs. Everyone argues against a world policeman's role for the United States; everyone also has a pet injustice somewhere in the world which he believes should be made an exception to the general rule. The problem is that if we would add up all the exceptions the United States would in fact be trying to play a world policeman's role.

To intervene into morally ambiguous situations, far removed from one's own culture and history and therefore little understood, is to become the neighborhood busybody. The world hardly needs the United States, or any other nation, telling everyone else how to run their affairs. Our own record of racism, economic injustices, political corruption and ravaging of the natural environment leaves us little room for moral superiority. The moral arrogance implicit in the concept of American intervention to correct alleged injustices of other nations is all too clear.

An additional factor arguing against a general right of intervention in cases of alleged wrongs is that the prior section and the principles defended there offer a basis for intervention based on justice and the God-given purpose of government. Under the standard enunciated there the United States is justified in intervening in foreign situations if necessary to protect the personal freedom of its own citizens. Since this intervention is to be done in keeping with justice toward other governments, it affords a basis for the United States to be actively involved in world affairs in a positive, justice-promoting manner, while at the same time stopping short of a morally arrogant interventionism.

In 1973, for example, the United States intervened in the outbreak of war between Israel and her Arab neighbors in the form of arms supplies to Israel and pressures on both sides to reach a peace settlement. This intervention could be justified on the basis of safeguarding justice and personal freedom within the United States. The involvement of the Soviet Union and its attempt to thereby expand its influence in the Middle East, as well as the presence of Middle Eastern oil on which the United States is becoming increasingly dependent, made the Middle Eastern situation directly relevant to the United States and the future well-being of Americans. Thus actions aimed at attaining peace in the Middle East, by helping to assure the continued flow of oil to the United States and preventing undue Soviet influence in the area, helps to protect the freedom of Americans. Thus American intervention in a situation such as this is fully justified. But what must also be remembered in this example is that this intervention must respect the rights of both the Arab nations and Israel. For the United States to intervene to support either side conquering the other side, destroying governments and making the people subject to them, while perhaps helping to guarantee the freedom of Americans, would have been wrong. We then would not have been respecting the rights of the nations involved. Thus American intervention in a situation such as this must take justice and national rights into account. To the extent it does, American intervention will help to overcome injustice and inhumanities in the world.

In short, it can be argued that intervention based on the protection of a nation's own people's freedom and a respect for the rights of other nations allows for intervention in some circumstances, yet places limitations on intervention. It allows the United States to play an active role in the world, while offering a guideline which, if applied, will prevent promiscuous interventionism. Thus I am strongly tempted to conclude that no government has a right to intervene in other governments' international disputes or internal affairs except to protect its own citizens' true freedom (that is, to promote a just order among its citizens).

But this is not yet the full story. There are additional factors which suggest that there indeed is a right of intervention which goes beyond merely protecting the freedom of a government's own citizens. Admittedly, as argued above, the standards of protecting one's own citizens and treating other governments with justice does offer a basis for an active, humane role for the United States in the world. But limiting American involvement to this alone would prevent American involvement in some situations of gross injustice or appalling human suffering. The problem lies in the fact that the pursuit of justice by the American government as it relates to domestic affairs means the maximization of human freedom in its fullest and richest sense. But the pursuit of justice by the American government as it relates to foreign affairs means respecting the rights of other governments, which leaves untouched many basic human tragedies and sufferings occurring within those nations.

Yet to argue that the American government should go beyond this and show justice not only to foreign governments but also to all people everywhere is clearly unac-

205

ceptable, since this would require the United States to become a world government or at the very least the world's policeman. Neither our power nor our wisdom is sufficient for this.

Still, to argue that the United States has no right to intervene in international and foreign situations except to protect Americans' freedom is equally unacceptable to the morally sensitive Christian. For then there would be no basis for American involvement in the face of a natural disaster which makes thousands homeless and threatened with starvation, or of a savage war which, while unlikely to affect Americans, is taking thousands or even hundreds of thousands of lives, or of a vicious, totalitarian regime which is using terror and extermination against sections of its population. To argue that the United States must always sit by as tragedies such as these occur is to argue that available influence, which could be used to reduce human suffering, is not to be used.

Perhaps a parallel can be drawn between two families living on the same block. Each one basically owes the other a respect which keeps each one from violating the rights of the other and from intervening in the personal affairs of the other. I am not to steal my neighbor's garden hose nor to tell him how to raise his children. In the same way one government is to show respect to another government by not violating its rights or intervening in its internal affairs. This much was developed in the prior section.

But in the case of neighbors intervention is sometimes justified and even required, as in the case of a natural disaster such as a fire or of a break-in by thieves or of physical abuse of the children by a drunken father. The condition necessary for intervention in such instances is that the harm which is threatening or affecting my neighbor must be truly severe and irreparable. Intervention is a last resort, reserved for unusually extenuating circumstances.

Normally my love for my neighbor leads me to respect his privacy and his self-reliance. Departure from this norm is to be tolerated only under extreme circumstances. It is only then that my moral obligation to help those in need takes precedence over my moral obligation to respect the privacy and self-reliance of my neighbor. Otherwise I become a moral busybody.

One can argue that a parallel exists between the neighbor in severe need and the people of another country in severe need—whether the need is caused by foreign military invasion, natural disaster or an unjust, repressive government. After all, national distinctions are essentially artificial. Christianity teaches the worth and dignity of all men, based on their all being created by God in his image. Thus my obligation extends to all men. It does not stop at national boundaries. The conclusion appears inescapable: One people has an obligation to help another people when they are dying from floods, drought or other natural disasters, are being slaughtered by a foreign invader, or are being repressed and enslaved by their own government. Christian love would seem to demand no less. Yet the specter of a morally arrogant interventionism causes the morally humble Christian to draw back.

We are thereby driven to the conclusion that, if we are to avoid both an unlimited interventionism and a cold indifference, on some occasions and under some circumstances one government has the right, even the obligation, to go beyond acting with justice toward other governments and to act to relieve human pain and suffering. To sort out what those occasions and circumstances are which justify and require the exertion of American influence and aid is the challenge.

A partial answer to that challenge seeks to take three factors into account, giving each its due weight. The first is the seriousness or the depth of the injustice or disaster.

British treatment of the Catholic minority in Northern Ireland, prejudicial though it may be, cannot be equated with Stalin's slaughter of hundreds of thousands (perhaps millions) of Ukrainians in the 1930s. A second factor is the form of intervention being suggested. It can take the form of material gifts and supplies at one extreme and armed military intervention on the other. In between lies a series of gradations: moral suasion and public criticism to mild economic sanctions to severe economic sanctions.

A third relevant factor which should be weighed is the extent to which the intervention being suggested is multinational in nature. Intervention can be unilateral, with one nation acting alone, or it can be multinational, with many nations of quite different regional, cultural, economic and ideological backgrounds acting together. The United States acting alone or in concert with one or two nations such as Canada or Britain with whom we share many regional, cultural, economic and ideological characteristics is quite different from a concert of fifty nations including European, African and Asian nations, western and non-western nations, developed and developing nations, democratic and communistic nations. In the latter case, with so many nations of such diverse backgrounds all agreeing that some other nation is perpetrating injustice, the case for some sort of action is much stronger than in the former case, with only a few nations of very similar background in agreement.

Figure 3 incorporates these three factors. The *form* of intervention is divided according to whether it is coercive—from armed intervention to economic sanctions—or non-coercive—from material aid to public condemnation and moral persuasion. The *degree* of injustice or human suffering involved is divided according to whether it is severe or mild. And the multinational or unilateral *nature* of the intervention is noted. Taking these three factors into ac-

| | Coercive Action | | Noncoercive Action | |
	mild injustice	severe injustice	mild injustice	severe injustice
multi-national action	probably no	probably yes	probably yes	definitely yes
uni-lateral action	definitely no	probably no	probably no	probably yes

figure 3

count, the figure indicates whether intervention is definitely or probably justified, or definitely or probably not justified.

The weakness of Figure 3 is that each of these three divisions is in reality a continuum, with an innumerable number of gradations in between the two extremes, whereas Figure 3 of necessity represents each as a simple dichotomy. Yet Figure 3 does bring these three factors together and demonstrates the relative justifiability of intervention depending on the combination of them. The more multinational the intervention, the more noncoercive the nature of the intervention, and the more severe the injustices which are being attacked, the more justifiable is the intervention. The more unilateral the intervention, the more coercive the intervention, and the more mild the injustices, the less justifiable is the intervention.

The principle illustrated by this scheme is not very neat and tidy. I wish I could draw the line between justifiable intervention and unjustifiable intervention more clearly. But honesty and reality do not allow me to do so. The real world is often like that. Difficult though the application of the principle illustrated here is, setting down the basic variables involved at least advances us beyond the person who has not even thought through the relevant variables and has unconsciously chosen to weigh the improper variables. The path to the proper application of this principle to specific questions of intervention and nonintervention is filled with dangers and pitfalls—and there will be disagreements—but we are at least headed down the right path. And judging from past errors and the often fuzzy thinking in this area, that is no small achievement.

BETWEEN OPTIMISM AND DESPAIR

The five ingredients of what I have called *progressive realism* seek to develop a Christian response to the problem of creating foreign policy stances in keeping with what God has revealed concerning man and his will for man, and are in keeping with what our observations tell us about the world of international politics. To tread the line between naive optimism and hopeless despair, between moral arrogance and cold indifference, is not easy. The five ingredients discussed here do not reveal the exact location of that line. But they do recognize its existence and suggest some basic approaches with which to search for it.

And in many ways that is what this entire book is all about. It is not a political program. It is not a blueprint for the construction of a political program. What it is, is a very personal attempt to point out some basic implications of the perspectives on man and politics revealed by God in his Word. It is only as Christ lives in us and freely gives us his grace that we will have the wisdom, humility and boldness needed to grasp the relevant principles and apply them to an onrushing world. In the process we must define for ourselves, taking into account the situations in which God has placed us, the line between right and wrong, wisdom and folly, naivete and vision, realism and despair.

Notes

Chapter 1

[1]David Halberstam, *The Best and the Brightest* (New York: Random House, 1972), pp. 38-39.

[2]Arthur M. Schlesinger, Jr., *The Crisis of Confidence* (Boston: Houghton, Mifflin, 1969), p. ix.

[3]"Second Thoughts About Man," *Time*, April 2, 1973, p. 78.

[4]Charles A. Reich, *The Greening of America* (New York: Random House, 1970).

[5]Alvin Toffler, *Future Shock* (New York: Random House, 1970).

[6]Richard Bach, *Jonathan Livingston Seagull* (New York: Macmillan, 1970).

[7]See *Newsweek*, December 10, 1973, pp. 40-45.

[8]Based on a continuing study of trust in government by the Center for Political Studies, University of Michigan.

[9]The accuracy of the claim that the failures of our politics—and therefore the path to renewal—lie in society's assumptions, beliefs and ideals will be demonstrated in subsequent chapters. Especially in parts II and III where I deal with specific public policies, I seek to show how the assumptions, beliefs and ideals of the right, left and new left have led to our current policy failures, and how the assumptions, beliefs and ideals of Christianity offer a better way.

[10]Fundamentalism is a term also sometimes used to refer to this branch of Christianity. But fundamentalism was essentially an early twentieth-century phenomenon which arose in reaction to attacks by theological liberals on the authority of the Bible and many orthodox Christian doctrines. It developed

an anti-intellectualism and a rigid, legalistic approach to personal ethics. Although orthodox, evangelical Christianity shares with fundamentalism most of the basic Christian doctrines, it is distinguishable from fundamentalism by its intellectual emphasis and less legalistic approach to personal ethics. On the distinction between evangelical Christianity and fundamentalism see William E. Hordern, *A Layman's Guide to Protestant Theology*, 2nd ed. (New York: Macmillan, 1968), pp. 54-56; J. I. Packer, *"Fundamentalism" and the Word of God* (Grand Rapids: Eerdmans, 1958), chap. 2; and Carl F. H. Henry, *Evangelical Responsibility in Contemporary Theology* (Grand Rapids: Eerdmans, 1957), chap. 2. For more complete discussions of the basic beliefs of historic, evangelical Christianity see Edward John Carnell, *The Case for Orthodox Theology* (Philadelphia: Westminster, 1959), pp. 33-50, 66-80; C. S. Lewis, *Mere Christianity* (New York: Macmillan, 1958), pp. 29-51; and Packer, *"Fundamentalism" and the Word of God*, chaps. 3—5.

[11]For discussions of orthodoxy, liberalism and neo-orthodoxy see Hordern, *A Layman's Guide*, and Bernard Ramm, *A Handbook of Contemporary Theology* (Grand Rapids: Eerdmans, 1966).

[12]Hordern, *A Layman's Guide*, p. 72.

Chapter 2

[1]Genesis 1:27. That the concept of the image of God in man is of central importance in the biblical view of man is indicated by the fact that it is also referred to in Genesis 1:26 and numerous other places in the Bible, such as Genesis 5:1, Ephesians 4:24 and Colossians 3:10.

[2]See G. C. Berkouwer, *Man: The Image of God* (Grand Rapids: Eerdmans, 1962), p. 77; and James Orr, *God's Image in Man* (London: Hodder and Stoughton, 1905), pp. 59-66.

[3]David G. Mandelbaum, "Cultural Anthropology," in the *International Encyclopedia of the Social Sciences*, ed. David L. Sills (New York: Macmillan and Free Press, 1968), I, 313. Also see Walter Goldschmidt, *Man's Way* (New York: Holt, Rinehart and Winston, 1959), pp. 17-30.

[4]For a thorough discussion of the development and history of the concept of culture see Milton Singer, "Culture: The Concept of Culture," in the *International Encyclopedia of the Social Sciences*, XIII, 527-40.

[5]This is not meant to imply that man can be absolutely distinguished from all animals by all four of these characteristics. Some sort of parallel can be found in the animal world for all four of these characteristics. What distinguishes man is the much higher, much more sophisticated level on which these four characteristics are found in man. Some primates, for example, make tools from pieces of wood with which to dig for grubs; man makes computers and spaceships.

[6]Edmund W. Sinnott, "The Creativeness of Life," in *Creativity and Its Cultivation*, ed. Harold Anderson (New York: Harper and Row, 1959), p. 12.

[7]Ibid., p. 21.

[8]Orr, *God's Image in Man*, p. 62.

[9]Morris has pointed out that it is the chimpanzee's lack of intelligence, not the lack of the necessary anatomical structures, that prevents him from speaking. See Desmond Morris, *The Naked Ape* (New York: McGraw-Hill, 1967), p. 113.

214

[10]See Konrad Lorenz, *On Aggression*, trans. Marjorie K. Wilson (New York: Harcourt, Brace, and World, 1966); Morris, *The Naked Ape*; Lionel Tiger and Robin Fox, *The Imperial Animal* (New York: Dell, 1971); and Robert Ardrey, *The Territorial Imperative* (New York: Dell, 1966).

[11]See Alexander Alland, Jr., *The Human Imperative* (New York: Columbia Univ. Press, 1972); George F. Kneller, *The Art and Science of Creativity* (New York: Holt, Rinehart and Winston, 1965); and the selections in *Creativity*, ed. Anderson.

[12]Kneller, *The Art and Science of Creativity*, p. 89.

[13]See Ronald Fletcher, *Instinct in Man* (New York: Schocken, 1966), pp. 17-22; and Goldschmidt, *Man's Way*, pp. 20-22.

[14]Goldschmidt, *Man's Way*, p. 18.

[15]See the story of a seagull that left the flock to learn new flying and diving skills. Bach, *Jonathan Livingston Seagull*.

[16]Genesis 1:28.

[17]Udo Middelmann, *Pro-Existence* (Downers Grove, Ill.: InterVarsity Press, 1974), p. 17. See chapters 1 and 2 of this book for an excellent discussion within a Christian framework of man's creative nature and the implications this creativity has for man's work.

[18]2 Corinthians 5:10.

[19]Reinhold Niebuhr, *The Nature and Destiny of Man* (New York: Scribner's, 1941), I, 162-63.

[20]Psychologist Abraham Maslow has written, "Self-actualizing creativeness is hard to define because sometimes it seems to be synonymous with health itself. And since self-actualization or health must ultimately be defined as the coming to pass of the fullest humanness, or as the 'Being' of the person, it is as if self-actualizing creativity were almost synonymous with, or a *sine quo non* of, or a defining characteristic of, essential humanness." Abraham H. Maslow, "Creativity in Self-Actualizing People," in *Creativity*, ed. Anderson, p. 94.

[21]C. S. Lewis, *Mere Christianity* (New York: Macmillan, 1958), p. 7.

[22]Reinhold Niebuhr, *Moral Man and Immoral Society* (New York: Scribner's, 1960), p. 37.

[23]Goldschmidt, *Man's Way*, p. 72.

[24]John Calvin, *Commentaries on the First Book of Moses Called Genesis* (Grand Rapids: Eerdmans, 1948), I, 94-95.

[25]René de Visme Williamson, *Independence and Involvement: A Christian Reorientation in Political Science* (Baton Rouge: Louisiana State Univ. Press, 1964), pp. 148-49.

[26]Matthew 22:37-39. Actually Jesus was in part quoting from the Old Testament book of Deuteronomy. See Deuteronomy 6:5.

[27]Romans 13:8-10.

[28]I Peter 4:8.

[29]1 Peter 4:10-11.

[30]Alland, *The Human Imperative*, p. 162.

[31]Quoted in John H. Hallowell, *Main Currents in Modern Political Thought* (New York: Holt, Rinehart and Winston, 1950), p. 168.

[32]Jean Jacques Rousseau, *The Social Contract and Discourses* (London: Dent, 1913), p. 214.

[33]Quoted in Hallowell, *Main Currents*, p. 389.

[34]Frank Podmore, *Robert Owen* (New York: Haskell House, 1971) [first published, 1907], II, 646-47.

[35]See Hallowell, *Main Currents*, pp. 439-42; and Lester De Koster, *Communism and Christian Faith* (Grand Rapids: Eerdmans, 1956), pp. 31-35.

[36]B. F. Skinner, *Beyond Freedom and Dignity* (New York: Knopf, 1971), p. 215.

[37]Ibid., p. 25.

[38]Ibid., pp. 213-14. Skinner, interestingly enough, while arguing that man's behavior is determined by his environment, argues that man in turn controls his own environment (see p. 215). In so doing he is caught in a net of his own making. For if man is totally a product of his environment, the absence or presence of a desire to change that environment (in order thereby to change behavior) must itself be a product of that environment. Man's cultural development thereby becomes an unalterable force, predetermined by the accidents of the specific environmental configurations of innumerable individuals.

[39]Mark 7:20-23. Also see the parallel account given in Matthew 15:18-20.

[40]James 1:14-15.

[41]Augustine, *City of God* (Garden City, N.Y.: Doubleday, 1958), p. 295.

[42]John Calvin, *Institutes of the Christian Religion* (Philadelphia: Westminster, 1960), I, 251.

[43]Harry R. Davis and Robert C. Good, eds., *Reinhold Niebuhr on Politics* (New York: Scribner's, 1960), p. 38.

[44]Quoted in George B. Lockwood, *The New Harmony Movement* (New York: Appleton, 1905), p. 175. A biographer of Owen wrote: "No one who has followed the course of his life can deny the reality of that vision, the unconquerable faith which it inspired. The disaster on disaster which overwhelmed one after another of his schemes for social salvation were to Owen but the momentary falling back of the waves as the tide flows up the beach..." (Podmore, *Robert Owen*, p. 646).

[45]See Morris Hillquit, *History of Socialism in the United States* (New York: Funk and Wagnalls, 1903), pp. 138-45.

[46]This admittedly does not respond directly to the behaviorist school of thought typified by Skinner. Since their methods have never been fully tried, there is no evidence one way or the other. The failures of other attempts to eradicate evil by manipulating environmental conditions would, however, seem to place the burden of proof on those who come up with yet another environmental approach to the eradication of evil.

[47]Lorenz, *On Aggression*, pp. xi and 241-46.

[48]Ibid., pp. 245-46.

[49]Tiger and Fox, *The Imperial Animal*, p. 238. Italics added.

[50]Lorenz, *On Aggression*, p. 299. Italics added.

[51]This approach has been taken by James Orr and many other Christian theologians. See Orr, *God's Image in Man*, p. 215.

[52]This was stressed by all the Protestant reformers. See Charles Hodge, *Systematic Theology* (Grand Rapids: Eerdmans, n.d.) [first published, 1871-73], II, 180-88.

[53]Matthew 22:37-40.

[54]Orr, *God's Image in Man*, pp. 216-17.

[55]Romans 1:29-31.

[56]Philippians 3:19.

[57]Reinhold Niebuhr holds to this position and quotes Augustine, Pascal, Aquinas, Luther and Calvin in support of it. See Niebuhr, *Nature and Destiny of Man*, pp. 186-87.

[58]Galatians 5:19-21.

[59]Calvin, *Institutes*, I, 292. For a good summary of Calvin's thought on the extent of man's corruption see Berkouwer, *Man*, pp. 148-52.

[60]Hodge, *Systematic Theology*, II, 233.

[61]See the development of this point by Berkouwer, *Man*, pp. 152-93.

[62]For a book which describes a tribal society marked by a depth of depravity and self-love and which thereby highlights the existence of a certain level of goodness and social love present in most societies, see Colin M. Turnbull, *The Bitter Silence of the Ik* (New York: Simon and Schuster, 1972).

Chapter 3

[1]James Madison, *The Federalist*, No. 51.

[2]For discussions of authority and legitimacy and their significance in political analysis see Robert A. Dahl, *Modern Political Analysis*, 2nd ed. (Englewood Cliffs, N.J.: Prentice-Hall, 1970), chap. 3; and Robert L. Peabody, "Authority," in the *Encyclopedia of the Social Sciences*, I, 473-77.

[3]Some governments are, of course, accorded very little legitimacy by their citizens. Such governments usually try to use increasing coercion to maintain themselves in power, but are normally highly unstable, falling victim to coups or revolutions.

[4]This approach is used by David Easton in his definition of the political system and has attained wide use among political scientists. See David Easton, *The Political System* (New York: Knopf, 1953), pp. 125-34.

[5]This is the sense in which the term is most frequently used by political scientists today. It ought not to be confused with partisanship, as is often done in popular American usage. Politics includes the competing of rival political parties for strength, but also includes all other processes that go to make up the actual decision-making processes of the government.

[6]Freedom and liberty are taken synonymously here, and I use the terms interchangeably in this book.

[7]In the following discussion most of the points and examples I utilize are most clearly applicable to limitations to human actions, in distinction from human speech or thoughts. And in fact our freedom of action is most easily limited and our freedom of thought least easily limited. For the most part, however, what follows applies to speech and thought as well as to acts.

[8]For a summary and critique of positivism's view of man see Hallowell, *Main Currents in Modern Political Thought*, pp. 289-327.

[9]See Hallowell, *Main Currents*, pp. 19-30, 60-67. The exact content of the rights inherent in man is a different question from the one being considered here. All that is being asserted at this point is that man does in fact possess certain inherent rights.

[10]See pp. 15-21 of the present volume.

[11]Whether and to what extent the government should be actively apportioning by its power these rights and their corresponding obligations is a separate question. The principles involved in that question are considered later in this chapter.

[12]Especially in the area of convenience rights or advantages, whether or not providing a particular right or advantage increases the sum total of personal freedom in a society is often in doubt. Difficult choices must often be made. Part III considers the entire question of the application of basic principles, such as this one, to ongoing, real-life situations.

[13]Not many persons have argued that a societal-wide order can be created by this means, but as will be seen in the following chapter persons have often argued that justice and order in a certain aspect of society can be achieved by this means.

[14]Mancur Olson, Jr., *The Logic of Collective Action* (New York: Schoken, 1968), p. 16.

[15]See pp. 36-38.

[16]See the discussion of this issue in Carl F. H. Henry, *The God Who Shows Himself* (Waco, Tex.: Word Books, 1966), chap. 4.

[17]The remaining chapters of the book are concerned with this very problem of applying the basic concepts developed in this and the preceding chapter to concrete, ongoing issues and situations.

[18]See Samuel Stouffer, *Communism, Conformity and Civil Liberties* (New York: Doubleday, 1955); and Herbert McClosky, "Consensus and Ideology in American Politics," *American Political Science Review*, 58 (1964), 361-82.

[19]See Stephen V. Monsma, "Potential Leaders and Democratic Values," *Public Opinion Quarterly*, 35 (1971), 350-57.

[20]Quoted in W. Lloyd Warner, Paul P. Van Riper, Norman H. Martin, and Orvis F. Collins, *The American Federal Executive* (New Haven: Yale Univ. Press, 1963), pp. 223-24.

[21]Quoted in Charles L. Clapp, *The Congressman: His Work as He Sees It* (Washington, D. C.: Brookings, 1963), p. 437.

Chapter 4

[1]For good summaries and critiques of traditional conservatism see Hallowell, *Main Currents in Modern Political Thought*, pp. 183-297; and George H. Sabine, *A History of Political Theory*, 3rd ed. (New York: Holt, Rinehart and Winston, 1961), pp. 617-19.

[2]Williamson, *Independence and Involvement*, p. 75.

[3]Edmund Burke, "Reflections on the Revolution in France," as quoted in Hallowell, *Main Currents*, p. 195.

[4]Romans 12:2.

[5]Williamson, *Independence and Involvement*, p. 81.

[6]For good summaries and critiques of classical liberal thought see Hallowell, *Main Currents*, pp. 84-117 and 135-58; and Williamson, *Independence and Involvement*, pp. 67-70.

[7]Sabine, *A History of Political Theory*, p. 532.

[8]Ibid., p. 529.

[9]In England a 1842 Parliamentary investigation of English coal mines "proved that children of five and six years of age and women labored under conditions fatal to health. Dragging and pushing carts along dangerously low and narrow subterranean passages, these people worked in places where beasts of burden could not. The report demonstrated that girls from eight to ten years old carried coal up ladders or steep stairways in heavy baskets

many times a day. A day could be thirteen hours for those children." Richard M. Brace, *The Making of the Modern World* (New York: Holt, Rinehart and Winston, 1955), p. 490.

[10]For good summaries of revisionist liberalism and democratic socialism see Hallowell, *Main Currents*, pp. 217-35, 277-88, 368-69 and 463-76; and Williamson, *Independence and Involvement*, pp. 89-97.

[11]Hallowell, *Main Currents*, p. 234.

[12]Ibid., p. 368.

[13]Sabine, *A History of Political Theory*, p. 729.

[14]See Thomas Hill Green, "Liberal Legislation and Freedom of Contract," in *Works* (London: Longmans, Green, 1911), III, 365-86.

[15]See Sabine, *A History of Political Theory*, pp. 739-40.

[16]Barry Goldwater, *The Conscience of a Conservative* (New York: Hillman Books, 1960), pp. 16-17.

[17]Ibid., p. 17.

[18]Ibid., p. 11.

[19]Ibid., p. 11.

[20]Richard M. Nixon, "Inaugural Address," *U.S. News and World Report*, 66 (February 3, 1969), 78.

[21]Ibid., 79.

[22]William F. Buckley, "On the Right," *National Review*, February 16, 1973, p. 227.

[23]Quoted in James K. Batten, "Sam Ervin and the Privacy Invaders," *The New Republic*, May 8, 1971, p. 20.

[24]See pp. 45-48.

[25]The death rate in American mines is considerably higher than in other modern, industrialized countries. See Ben A. Franklin, "The Scandal of Death and Injury in the Mines," *New York Times Magazine*, March 30, 1969, pp. 25-27, 122-30; and Duane Lockard, *The Perverted Priorities of American Politics* (New York: Macmillan, 1971), pp. 6-13.

[26]See pp. 58-59.

[27]For evidence that this is, in fact, the case see Richard V. Pierard, *The Unequal Yoke* (Philadelphia: Lippincott, 1970), pp. 15-25; and David O. Moberg, *The Great Reversal* (Philadelphia: Lippincott, 1972), pp. 46-66.

[28]Kenneth G. Elzinga, "The Demise of Capitalism and the Christian Response," *Christianity Today*, July 7, 1972, p. 963.

[29]See Matthew 7:13-14.

[30]He made this statement in March, 1972, in his concession speech upon losing the Florida primary.

[31]Michael Harrington, *Toward a Democratic Left* (New York: Macmillan, 1968), p. 30.

[32]Robert A. Dahl, *After the Revolution?* (New Haven: Yale Univ. Press, 1970), p. 114.

[33]Ramsey Clark, *Crime in America* (New York: Simon and Schuster, 1970), p. 19.

[34]Ibid., p. 43.

[35]In addition to the following references see Reo M. Christenson, *Heresies Right and Left: Some Political Assumptions Re-examined* (New York: Harper and Row, 1973); Richard C. Cornuelle, *Reclaiming the American Dream* (New York: Random House, 1965); Daniel P. Moynihan, *Maximum Feasible Misunderstanding* (New York: Free Press, 1969); Halberstam, *The Best and the*

Brightest; and Theodore J. Lowi, *The End of Liberalism* (New York: Norton, 1969).

[36]Dahl, *After the Revolution?* p. 128.

[37]Peter Drucker, *The Age of Discontinuity* (New York: Harper and Row, 1969), p. 212.

[38]Halberstam, *The Best and the Brightest*, p. 44.

[39]Moynihan, *Maximum Feasible Misunderstanding*, pp. xii-xiii.

[40]For those who doubt this statement see Nathan Glazar, "Introduction," in Stanley M. Elkins, *Slavery* (New York: Grosset and Dunlop, 1963).

[41]*Webster's Seventh New Collegiate Dictionary* (Springfield, Mass.: Merriam, 1967), p. 530.

[42]See p. 56.

[43]Moynihan, *Maximum Feasible Misunderstanding*, pp. xv-xvi.

[44]On the tendency of liberal government policies to reinforce already existing social conditions, see Lowi, *The End of Liberalism*, pp. 58-67.

[45]Ibid., p. 101.

[46]For confirmation of this point see Walton Hamilton, *The Politics of Industry* (New York: Knopf, 1957); Marver Bernstein, *Regulating Business by Independent Commission* (Princeton, N.J.: Princeton Univ. Press, 1955); Louis M. Kohlmeier, *The Regulators* (New York: Harper and Row, 1969), chap. 6; and Robert C. Fellmeth, *The Interstate Commerce Omission: The Public Interest and the ICC* (New York: Grossman, 1970).

[47]See Lowi, *The End of Liberalism*, pp. 125-56.

[48]For summaries of these bills see *Congressional Quarterly Almanac, 1971* (Washington, D.C.: Congressional Quarterly Service, 1972), pp. 175-78 and 472-86.

[49]In June of 1962 the then fledgling Students for a Democratic Society met at Port Huron, Michigan, and adopted a statement drafted by Tom Hayden which set down the basic theories and goals of the SDS at that time. See Students for a Democratic Society, *The Port Huron Statement* (New York: Students for a Democratic Society, 1964), p. 7.

[50]Quoted in "Portrait of a Young Radical," *Newsweek*, September 30, 1968, pp. 66-67.

[51]Quoted in Garry Wills, *Nixon Agonistes* (New York: New American Library, 1969), p. 342.

[52]SDS, *Port Huron Statement*, cover and p. 7.

[53]Ibid., p. 6.

[54]Herbert Marcuse, "Repressive Tolerance," in Robert P. Wolff, Barrington Moore, Jr., and Herbert Marcuse, *A Critique of Pure Tolerance* (Boston: Beacon, 1965), pp. 109-10. On the antidemocratic tendencies of the new left also see the discussion of Arthur M. Schlesinger, Jr., *The Crisis of Confidence* (Boston: Houghton, Mifflin, 1969), pp. 36-46.

[55]Howard Zinn, *Disobedience and Democracy* (New York: Random House, 1968).

[56]Marcuse, "Repressive Tolerance," pp. 116-17.

[57]Reich, *The Greening of America*, p. 4.

[58]National Advisory Commission on Civil Disorders, *Report* (New York: Bantam, 1968), p. 1.

[59]For an able review and critique of the new left movement from a Christian perspective see Os Guinness, *The Dust of Death* (Downers Grove, Ill.: InterVar-

sity Press, 1973).

[60]Quoted in Guinness, *The Dust of Death*, p. 109.

[61]I do not mean to imply that the entire new left movement was marked by violent and repressive tendencies. The movement has many different factions and facets. Some did not espouse violence and the denial of civil rights, but others did.

Chapter 5

[1]On the concept of political culture see Lucian W. Pye, "Political Culture," in the *International Encyclopedia of the Social Sciences*, XII, 218-25 and Donald J. Devine, *The Political Culture of the United States* (Boston: Little, Brown, 1972), pp. 1-18.

[2]Robert E. Ward, "Political Modernization and Political Culture in Japan," in Claude E. Welch, Jr., *Political Modernization* (Belmont, Calif.: Wadsworth, 1967), p. 92. Originally published in *World Politics*, 15 (1963), 569-96.

[3]See David E. Apter, "The Role of Traditionalism in the Political Modernization of Ghana and Uganda," *World Politics*, 12 (1960), 45-68.

[4]See Gabriel Almond and Sidney Verba, *The Civic Culture* (Princeton, N.J.: Princeton Univ. Press, 1963).

[5]Devine, *The Political Culture*, p. 11.

[6]See Kenneth P. Langton, *Political Socialization* (New York: Oxford Univ. Press, 1969); and James J. Best, *Public Opinion* (Homewood, Ill.: Dorsey, 1973), chap. 3.

[7]See pp. 24-38.

[8]Although it must be remembered that Christianity teaches that it is only through the grace of God that men reach such levels of goodness. See earlier, p. 38.

[9]See Colin M. Turnbull, *The Mountain People* (New York: Simon and Schuster, 1972).

[10]See chapter 3, pp. 52-56, for the development of the crucial and paradoxical point that true personal freedom, and therefore the maximization of true personal freedom, emerges from the proper balancing of free choice and limitations on free choice. Thus when I write here of maximizing true freedom I am not speaking of every man doing his own thing in some sort of an anarchistic-like situation. Rather I am referring to the careful balancing of rights and obligations, advantages and disadvantages, freedom and limitations on freedom, out of which we all are made more free. This, I argued in chapter 3, is the defining characteristic of justice or a just order.

[11]James 5:1-4.

[12]See *Congressional Quarterly Almanac, 1972* (Washington, D.C.: Congressional Quarterly Service, 1973), p. 770.

[13]Enid Nemy, "Hair Fairy Visits Leukemia Youngster," *The Grand Rapids Press*, March 4, 1973, p. 15-E.

[14]See American Friends Service Committee, *Struggle for Justice* (New York: Hill and Wang, 1971), pp. 91-92.

[15]American Friends Service Committee, *Struggle for Justice*, p. 96. For a good summary of the literature attacking rehabilitation as inhumane see Stuart Barton Babbage, "C. S. Lewis and the Humanitarian Theory of Punishment,"

Christian Scholars Review, 2 (1972), 224-35.

[16]See American Friends Service Committee, *Struggle for Justice*, p. 91; and Eve Pell, ed., *Maximum Security* (New York: Dutton, 1972), p. 18.

[17]American Friends Service Committee, *Struggle for Justice*, p. 25.

[18]Jessica Mitford, *Kind and Usual Punishment* (New York: Knopf, 1973), p. 103.

[19]C. S. Lewis, *God in the Dock* (Grand Rapids: Eerdmans, 1970), p. 293.

[20]See American Friends Service Committee, *Struggle for Justice*, pp. 91-92.

[21]See, for example, Robert A. Dahl and Charles E. Lindblom, *Politics, Economics, and Welfare* (New York: Harper, 1953); and Charles E. Lindblom, *The Policy-Making Process* (Englewood Cliffs, N.J.: Prentice-Hall, 1968).

[22]Lindblom, *The Policy-Making Process*, p. 27. For a more extended discussion by Lindblom of this contention see D. Braybrooke and C. E. Lindblom, *A Strategy of Decision* (New York: Free Press, 1963).

[23]Walton Hamilton, *The Politics of Industry* (New York: Knopf, 1957), p. 62. On the tendencies of administrative agencies to succumb to the influence of special interests see the references cited in footnote 46 of the previous chapter.

[24]See p. 105.

[25]This is a very typical pattern in the American bureaucracy. See, for example, Fellmeth, *The Interstate Commerce Omission*.

Chapter 6

[1]For a very helpful discussion of the three factors I mention here as contributing to the world's interdependence see Lester R. Brown, *World Without Borders* (New York: Random House, 1972).

[2]See p. 44.

[3]Austin Ranney, *The Governing of Men*, 3rd ed. (New York: Holt, Rinehart and Winston, 1971), p. 569.

[4]See pp. 39-40 and 70.

[5]Edward M. Kennedy, "Ulster Is an International Issue," *Foreign Policy*, No. 11 (Summer 1973), pp. 69-70.

[6]See my earlier discussion of American conservatism and its roots, pp. 85-89. On the conservative tradition in American foreign policy see the helpful discussion by Kenneth W. Thompson, *Political Realism and the Crisis of World Politics* (Princeton, N.J.: Princeton Univ. Press, 1960), pp. 70-90.

[7]Isaiah 40:17.

[8]George F. Kennan, "World Problems in Christian Perspective," *Theology Today*, 16 (July 1959), 156. The Dutch evangelical, Andre Donner, has summarized the Christian outlook towards national differences in this way: "We are taught to disregard national barriers, and to concentrate on the brotherhood of men, who have been created out of one blood." Andre Donner, *The Christian and the Nations* (Grand Rapids: Eerdmans, 1968), p. 17.

[9]For a good summary of idealism and realism see David C. Jordan, *World Politics in Our Time* (Lexington, Mass.: Heath, 1970), pp. 57-66.

[10]On idealism's optimistic view of man see Kenneth W. Thompson, *Christian Ethics and the Dilemmas of Foreign Policy* (Durham, N.C.: Duke Univ., 1959), pp. 117-22.

[11]F. S. C. Northrop, *The Taming of the Nations* (New York: Macmillan, 1954), p. 302.

[12]Ernest Lefever, *Ethics and United States Foreign Policy* (Cleveland: World, 1957), p. 22.

[13]On the dangers of moralism see Dean Acheson, "Morality, Moralism and Diplomacy," *The Yale Review*, 47 (Summer 1958), 481-93.

[14]Lefever, *Ethics*, p. 24.

[15]George F. Kennan, *Realities of American Foreign Policy* (Princeton, N.J.: Princeton Univ. Press, 1954), p. 48.

[16]James E. Dougherty and Robert L. Pfaltzgraff, *Contending Theories of International Relations* (Philadelphia: Lippincott, 1971), p. 66.

[17]One of the leading realist theoreticians, Hans Morgenthau, goes so far as to identify national interest with national power. See Hans J. Morgenthau, "Another 'Great Debate': The National Interest of the United States," *American Political Science Review*, 66 (December 1952), 961-88. Also see the excellent summary of Morgenthau's position in Dougherty and Pfaltzgraff, *Contending Theories*, pp. 75-80.

[18]Quoted in Thompson, *Political Realism*, p. 119.

[19]Arthur Schlesinger, Jr., "National Interests and Moral Absolutes," in *Ethics and World Politics*, ed. Ernest Lefever (Baltimore: Johns Hopkins Univ. Press, 1973), p. 29. Dougherty and Pfaltzgraff wrote: "Realists assume moral principles cannot be applied to political actions." Dougherty and Pfaltzgraff, *Contending Theories*, p. 66.

[20]Morgenthau, "Another 'Great Debate,' " p. 978.

[21]See Brown, *World Without Borders*, pp. 234-40.

[22]See Reo Christenson, *Heresies Right and Left* (New York: Harper and Row, 1973), pp. 175-78.

[23]John C. Bennett, *Foreign Policy in Christian Perspective* (New York: Scribner's, 1966), p. 60.

[24]Luke 12:48.

[25]See Schlesinger, "National Interests," p. 22, and the material quoted in footnote 19 above.

[26]Ibid., p. 26.

[27]This point is made by Arnold Wolfers, *Discord and Collaboration* (Baltimore: Johns Hopkins Univ. Press, 1962), pp. 47-65.

[28]Thomas I. Cook and Malcolm Moos, "The American Idea of International Interest," *American Political Science Review*, 67 (1953), 36.

[29]Ibid., p. 40.

[30]Quoted in Thompson, *Political Realism*, p. 18.

[31]See Brown, *World Without Borders*, pp. 336-37 and 350-55.

[32]Students for a Democratic Society, *Port Huron Statement*, p. 42.

[33]Brown, *World Without Borders*, p. 277.

[34]J. William Fulbright, *The Crippled Giant* (New York: Random House, 1972), pp. 274-75.

[35]Zbigniew Brzezinski, "U. S. Foreign Policy: The search for Focus," *Foreign Affairs*, July, 1973, p. 713.

[36]This is in keeping with the new left's tendencies toward simplifications (see chapter 4, p. 113) and moralism.

[37]Richard J. Barnet, *Roots of War* (New York: Atheneum, 1972), p. 5.

[38]Robert W. Tucker, *The Radical Left and American Foreign Policy* (Baltimore: Johns Hopkins Press, 1971), p. 12.

[39]See, for example, books such as Eugene McCarthy, *The Limits of Power* (New

York: Dell, 1967); and J. William Fulbright, *The Arrogance of Power* (New York: Random House, 1966).

[40]Fulbright, *The Crippled Giant*, p. 274.

[41]Brown, *World Without Borders*, p. 351.

[42]Fulbright, *The Crippled Giant*, pp. 164-65.

[43]Reinhold Niebuhr makes this contention at length in his *Moral Man and Immoral Society* (New York: Scribner's, 1932).

[44]Ibid., p. 93.

[45]See John E. Mueller, "Presidential Popularity from Truman to Johnson," *American Political Science Review,* 64 (1970), 21-22.

[46]Fulbright, *The Crippled Giant*, pp. 164-65.

[47]Goldwater, *Conscience*, pp. 91-92. Italics present.

[48]See ibid., pp. 102-18. It may be, of course, that Goldwater has modified his views since 1960. But his 1960 views stand as an example of conservatism-idealism, and his statement at the time Communist China was admitted to the United Nations calling for American withdrawal from the United Nations suggests his more recent views may not be all that different from what they were in 1960. See the *New York Times*, October 27, 1971, p. 16.

[49]Goldwater, *Conscience*, p. 105.

[50]See the *New York Times*, August 6, 1971, pp. 1 and 35.

[51]John A. Stormer, *None Dare Call It Treason* (Florissant, Mo.: Liberty Bell, 1964), p. 7.

[52]Quoted in John H. Redekop, *The American Far Right* (Grand Rapids: Eerdmans, 1968), p. 53.

[53]Billy James Hargis, *Communist America . . . Must It Be?* (Tulsa, Okla.: Christian Crusade, 1960), p. 173.

[54]See pp. 153-54.

[55]Mark O. Hatfield, in foreword to Redekop, *The American Far Right*, pp. 4-5.

[56]1 John 4:1.

[57]Alan F. Pater and Jason R. Pater, eds., *What They Said in 1972* (Beverly Hills, Calif.: Monitor Books, 1973), p. 27.

[58]Ibid., p. 27.

[59]Ibid., p. 26.

[60]Hans J. Morgenthau, *Politics Among Nations,* 2nd ed. (New York: Knopf, 1954), pp. 10-11.

[61]Ibid., p. 10.

[62]See, for example, Hans J. Morgenthau, *A New Foreign Policy for the United States* (New York: Praeger, 1969), chap. 5.

[63]See, for example, Morgenthau, *Politics Among Nations*, pp. 9-10.

[64]The terms are Morgenthau's. See ibid., p. 12.

[65]*Facts on File Yearbook, 1970* (New York: Facts on File, 1971), p. 298.

[66]Reinhold Niebuhr, *The Irony of American History* (New York: Scribner's, 1952), p. 40.

[67]Ibid., p. 148.

[68]Davis and Good, eds., *Reinhold Niebuhr on Politics* (New York: Scribner's, 1960), p. 65.

[69]Ibid., pp. 68-69.

[70]Edward M. Kennedy, *Decisions for a Decade* (Garden City, N.Y.: Doubleday, 1968), p. 204.

[71]Henry A. Kissinger, *American Foreign Policy* (New York: Norton, 1969), p. 94.

224

[72]Kennan, "World Problems in Christian Perspective," p. 168.

[73]Kennedy, *Decisions for a Decade*, p. 131. Kennedy's commitment to the desirability of American foreign policy's pursuing ideals and justice can also be seen in the earlier quotation of his on the Northern Ireland situation. See above, p. 151.

[74]Ibid., p. 138.

Chapter 7

[1]See pp. 160-61.

[2]See pp. 60-62.

[3]See Brown, *World Without Borders*, pp. 234-40, for an analysis of how the rich countries' trade policies systematically discriminate against the poor nations.

Index